MODERN WORLD NATIONS

P9-DFB-911

AFGHANISTAN	IRAN
ARGENTINA	IRAQ
AUSTRALIA	IRELAND
AUSTRIA	ISRAEL
BAHRAIN	ITALY
BERMUDA	JAPAN
BOLIVIA	KAZAKHSTAN
BRAZIL	KENYA
CANADA	KUWAIT
CHINA	MEXICO
COSTA RICA	THE NETHERLANDS
CROATIA	NEW ZEALAND
CUBA	NIGERIA
EGYPT	NORTH KOREA
ENGLAND	NORWAY
ETHIOPIA	PAKISTAN
FRANCE	PERU
REPUBLIC OF GEORGIA	RUSSIA
GERMANY	SAUDI ARABIA
GHANA	SCOTLAND
GUATEMALA	SOUTH AFRICA
ICELAND	SOUTH KOREA
INDIA	UKRAINE

MODERN WORLD NATIONS

Argentina

Richard A. Crooker

Kutztown University

Series Consulting Editor
Charles F. Gritzner
South Dakota State University

CHELSEA HOUSE
PUBLISHERS

A Haights Cross Communications Company

Frontispiece: Flag of Argentina

Cover: Cerro Torre in Patagonia, Argentina.

CHELSEA HOUSE PUBLISHERS

VP, NEW PRODUCT DEVELOPMENT Sally Cheney
DIRECTOR OF PRODUCTION Kim Shinners
CREATIVE MANAGER Takeshi Takahashi
MANUFACTURING MANAGER Diann Grasse

Staff for ARGENTINA

EXECUTIVE EDITOR Lee Marcott
PRODUCTION ASSISTANT Megan Emery
PICTURE RESEARCHER 21st Century Publishing and Communications, Inc.
SERIES DESIGNER Takeshi Takahashi
COVER DESIGNER Terry Mallon
LAYOUT 21st Century Publishing and Communications, Inc.

A Haights Cross Communications ⟋ Company

http://www.chelseahouse.com

First Printing

1 3 5 7 9 8 6 4 2

Library of Congress Cataloging-in-Publication Data applied for.

Crooker, Richard A.
   Argentina / by Richard A. Crooker
      p. cm.—(Modern world nations)
Includes bibliographical references and index.
   ISBN 0-7910-7480-3 (hardcover)   0-7910-7770-5 PB
   1. Argentina—Juvenile literature. I Title. II. Series.
F2808.2.C76 2003
982—dc21

                                        2003006921

Table of Contents

Argentina

Argentina is a long country, stretching about 2,300 miles (3,700 kilometers) from north to south. Ushuaia, shown here, is the southernmost town in Argentina—and the world.

Introducing Argentina

Argentina is a wedge-shaped country located in southeastern South America. People often refer to Argentina and its neighbors (Chile, Paraguay, and Uruguay) as the "Southern Cone," because South America resembles an ice cream cone. Physically, Argentina stands out in many ways. It is the second-largest country in South America. Only Brazil is larger among South American nations. In total area, it is the world's eighth-largest country. Argentina has the highest mountain peak (Mount Aconcagua) in the Western Hemisphere and the second-longest river (Paraná) in South America (the Amazon River is the longest). Argentina's capital, Buenos Aires, is the largest city in the Southern Cone.

The natural environment of Argentina is extremely varied. The country stretches about 2,300 miles (3,700 kilometers) from north to south. Consequently, the climate varies from hot and rainy in the north, to temperate in the middle, to cold and windswept in the south. Argentina has large expanses of desert area as well. Plant species range from orchids and tropical evergreen trees, to sub-polar flowers and southern beech. Magnificent grasslands have figured prominently in the development of the nation's agricultural economy. Many interesting and colorful animals thrive in the county's mountains, grasslands, deserts, forests, marshes, and coastal regions. They include llamas, armadillos, condors, and even penguins!

Argentina is different from most Latin American countries in one important way: about 90 percent of its population is of European ancestry. Few native people occupied the area when the Spanish arrived. Most of those who lived there either intermarried with European settlers, died of disease, or perished in wars with the settlers. Being mainly European, however, does not mean Argentina lacks cultural diversity. Although most Argentines are either Spanish or Italian, there are sizeable minority populations tracing their ancestors to the United Kingdom, Germany, France, Austria, Poland, Russia, and elsewhere. Some of these groups dominate the populations of certain towns and still prefer to speak their native language first and Spanish, which is the national language, second.

Argentina has its own distinct culture, despite the strong European influence. The country is probably best known for Buenos Aires (its capital), tango (a dance), *yerba maté* (a tea), *asado* (a beef barbeque), and *gauchos* (Argentine cowboys).

Argentines are Latin America's most highly urbanized people. About 85 percent of people live in cities. Yet the image of a *gaucho* on horseback is among the most important cultural symbols shared by Argentines. The Pampas,

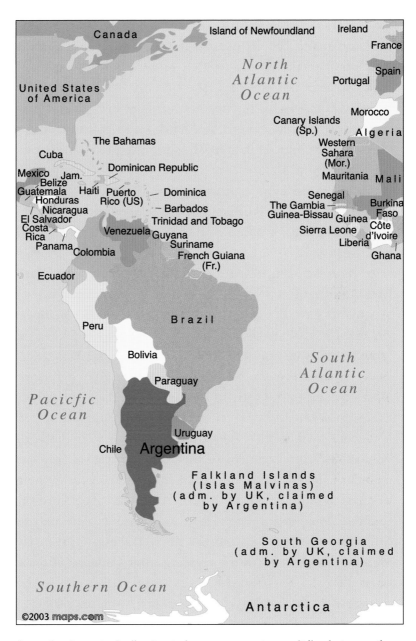

Canada   Island of Newfoundland   Ireland
France

*North
Atlantic
Ocean*
Portugal   Spain

United States
of America

Morocco
Canary Islands
(Sp.)   Algeria

The Bahamas   Western
Sahara
(Mor.)

Cuba

Mexico   Jam.   Dominican Republic   Mauritania   Mali
Belize
Guatemala   Haiti   Puerto   Dominica   Senegal   Burkina
Honduras   Rico (US)   The Gambia   Faso
Nicaragua   Barbados   Guinea-Bissau   Guinea   Côte
El Salvador   Trinidad and Tobago   Sierra Leone   d'Ivoire
Costa   Venezuela Guyana   Liberia
Rica   Suriname   Ghana
Panama Colombia   French Guiana
(Fr.)

Ecuador

Peru   *B r a z i l*

*South
Atlantic
Ocean*

Bolivia

*Pacicfic
Ocean*   Paraguay

Uruguay
Chile   **Argentina**

Falkland Islands
(Islas Malvinas)
(adm. by UK, claimed
by Argentina)

South Georgia
(adm. by UK, claimed
by Argentina)

Southern Ocean

Antarctica

©2003 maps.com

Argentina is strategically situated on ocean routes, as it lies between the Atlantic and Pacific Oceans. Its area of 1.1 million square miles (2.8 million square kilometers), second in Latin America only to that of Brazil, is about one-third the area of the United States without Alaska and Hawaii.

Argentina's rich agricultural region, has the densest network of roads and railroads in South America. Economic ties between the nation's cities, towns, and villages have helped keep the country together during its turbulent history. Historically, Buenos Aires copied European trends in culture. It is the most influential city in the country and the intellectual center of South America. Argentina benefits from rich natural resources, a well-educated population, an export-oriented agricultural sector, and a diversified industrial base. In addition, Argentina is strategically situated on ocean routes between the Atlantic and Pacific oceans.

Spain was the first to colonize Argentina. The word *Argentina* comes from a Latin word meaning "silvery." Spaniards gave the colony its name because they believed incorrectly that its rivers contained silver. (They knew of rich silver deposits in the Andes, in which the rivers originate.) Eventually, the Spanish Crown designated Buenos Aires the capital of part of its empire in the New World. The region languished during its colonial history, however. Independence, British investments, and new methods of transportation developed in the 19th century spurred the economy. By the early 20th century, Buenos Aires became known as the "Paris of South America." The country became a major supplier of beef and wheat to Europe and other parts of the world. At the time, Argentina's economy rivaled that of many other wealthy nations. Buenos Aires is still famous as an intellectual and cultural center. Moreover, trade and agriculture remain the backbone of Argentina's economy.

Poor leadership and great differences in regional and individual wealth have plagued Argentina throughout history. Today, its economy continues to be in a downward spiral that has lasted for more than half a century. Nevertheless, there are hopeful signs that Argentina can return to better economic times. In this book, you will learn how geography and history converged to create the modern nation of Argentina.

The Andes run along the entire western border of Argentina. The mountains shown here are in Salta Province in the northwestern part of the country.

Physical Landscapes

A rgentina's scenery is as magnificent as it is diverse. Rugged mountains and expansive plains and plateaus are home to an abundance of plants and animals. The country includes a variety of landscapes in four major physical regions: Andes, Pampas, Northeast, and Patagonia. Each region is an interrelated grouping of landforms, climates, and ecosystems.

THE ANDES

The Andes are a system of imposing north–south trending mountain ranges that form Argentina's western and northern border. Their rugged natural beauty rivals that of Europe's Alps. Jagged Andean peaks extend along the entire western coast of South America, including the length of Argentina from the Bolivian border in the north to Tierra del Fuego, an island at the southern tip of South America.

Argentina's northern Andes are a continuation of the Bolivian *altiplano* (Spanish for "high plain"). The *altiplano* is between 11,000 and 13,000 feet (3,350 to 4,000 meters) in elevation. Cone-shaped volcanoes and narrow mountain ranges stand high above its generally level surface, reaching 19,000 feet (5,800 meters) in some places. Argentina's southern Andes have higher peaks and more rugged topography than does the *altiplano*. Dominating the view in all directions are deep canyons, as well as towering summits.

Geologists refer to the Andes as youthful mountains because they are still rising. A collision of tectonic plates, or sections of Earth's lithosphere (outer rock layer), is causing the Andean buildup. The collision involves a large, westward-moving South America plate and three smaller plates that are moving eastward. The advancing edges of the smaller plates are going beneath the South America plate and melting to form magma (molten rock). The collision causes the western edge of South America to uplift and crumble into spectacular folded mountains. The peaks of the Andes are higher than any other mountains except the Himalayas of India and Tibet.

The magma forming beneath the continent forms explosive volcanoes—the Andes' highest peaks. Argentina's Mount Aconcagua is such a volcano. At 22,835 feet (6,960 meters), it is the highest peak in the Western Hemisphere. The country's western border with Chile has about 1,800 volcanoes. Volcanologists (scientists who study volcanoes) believe about 28 of them are still active. The last major volcanic eruption was in 1991 in the southern province of Santa Cruz. The eruption did not cause deaths, but 2,000 people were forced to temporarily evacuate their homes. The stress and strain of plate collision also cause faults (breaks) in Earth's crust and result in earthquakes (movements along the faults). The only major earthquake since 1975 took place in Mendoza Province. It destroyed many buildings, leaving more than 4,500 people homeless.

The climate of the Argentine Andes is varied. The mountains form a high wall, blocking moisture-bearing storms from the Pacific Ocean from entering Argentina. Most of the precipitation falls in Chile on the western side of the Andes. As a result, the climate of most of the Argentine Andes is semiarid (not quite desert), and most of the precipitation falls as snow. The highest elevations have an alpine (high mountain) climate. Temperatures are below freezing much of the year. Only mosses, lichens, and annual flowering plants survive the cold temperatures. The area between 46 and 51 degrees south latitude is high enough and moist enough to support Argentina's only glaciers. Most Andean glaciers that formed during the last Ice Age have since disappeared.

Most Andean soils are thin and infertile. Those in the low-elevation basins and mountain base valleys, however, are an exception. The natural vegetation is adapted to thin soils, low precipitation levels, and cold temperatures. The higher elevations have a scattering of cold-tolerant, widely spaced shrubs and grasses. Trees are only able to survive at lower elevations, below 6,000 feet (1,828 meters), where temperatures are warmer. A rare, dense forest thrives on the *altiplano's* eastern slope. It receives moist easterly winds blowing from the Atlantic Ocean. There is enough rainfall here to support a thin band of forest. Botanists (plant scientists) call this narrow evergreen forest the *Ceja de la montaña* (Spanish for "eyebrow of the forest"). In the southern Andes, two unique trees exist. The first is the Araucaria pine. This conifer tree provides nuts that have long been an important food source for the Native Americans in the region. The other tree is the southern beech. These two trees combine to form small areas of scattered, mixed woodlands in the southern Andes and neighboring areas of western Patagonia.

The only escape from the Andes' dryness and coldness is found in the bottomlands of canyons and basins along the eastern edge of the mountains. Here, farmers have taken

Argentina includes a number of landscapes in four physical regions: Andes, Pampas, Northeast, and Patagonia. Each region is an interrelated group of soils, vegetation types, climates, and landforms.

advantage of the relatively mild climate and fertile soils. Mountain towns such as Salta, Tucumán, Catamarca, La Rijoa, and Mendoza are important trade centers in these areas. The piedmont (foot of mountain) towns attract many visitors because of their cultural and historical importance. Visitors also come to enjoy the beauty of the glaciers and volcanoes. Some of the activities that draw visitors include camping, fishing, hiking, mountaineering, water skiing, snow skiing, water rafting, horseback riding, and paragliding.

Argentines depend on the Andes' natural resources. Meltwater from snow and ice feed the country's rivers. Hydroelectric dams on several of these rivers supply electricity to many regions of Argentina. Mining of small iron ore deposits and drilling of oil also contribute to the national economy.

PAMPAS

A second major physical region of Argentina is the Pampas. The Pampas are a huge expanse of grassy plains. They range in a broad semicircle from the coastal town of Bahia Blanca to the base of the Andes, thence to Santa Fe, and finally to the mouth of the Uruguay River. Windblown Andean glacial deposits have given the Pampas its flat surface and fertile soil. The Andes had more and larger glaciers during the last period of glaciations, which ended about 15,000 years ago. These glaciers and their meltwaters moved huge amounts of sediment to the base of the Andes. Winds blowing across the glacial deposits picked up fine, silt-size particles and carried them east to form thick deposits in the Pampas. Scientists call windblown deposits *loess*. The top layer of the loess has weathered to become a very rich soil that is the most productive in South America.

The Pampas have mild temperatures that are relatively cool in the summer and warm in the winter. Buenos Aires is a good example. The average temperature of the warmest month (January) is a comfortable 75°F (24°C). The average temperature of the coolest month (July) is a pleasant 50°F (10°C). Mild temperatures are typical throughout the Pampas. Storms distribute rainfall unevenly. There is a wetter eastern part, the humid Pampa, and a drier western part, the dry Pampa. The humid Pampa centers on Buenos Aires and Rosario. Both cities receive about 40 inches (1,000 millimeters) of rainfall annually. Bahia Blanca typifies the dry Pampa. Its annual rainfall amounts to about 24 inches (600 millimeters)—30 percent less than the humid Pampa.

The lifting and cooling of warm, moist air causes rain, snow, and hail. There are two types of rainstorms in the Pampas. In the summer (December, January, and February), surface heating causes convectional storms. During Argentina's summer, the land area heats up, making the overlying air lighter. The light-weight air rises, causing a low surface pressure system to develop. A steady moist southeast wind blows from the Atlantic Ocean to "fill" the low pressure. As the moist ocean wind moves over the hot land surface, it too heats up, rises, cools, and creates dark, moisture-laden clouds and convective rainstorms over the Pampas. About half of the summer convectional storms are accompanied by thunder, lightning, and sometimes hail. The violent summer thunderstorm and its brilliant display of lightning is a common sight in the Pampas region.

During the winter, an entirely different type of storm system occurs—frontal storms. They are triggered by cold dense air moving northward from Patagonia. Meteorologists (scientists who study weather) call the leading edge of a cold air mass a cold front. The cold front pushes against warm moist ocean air that already sits over the Pampas. The cold air is heavier than warm air, so the warm air spirals upward as the cold air pushes against it. As the warm air rises, it cools and forms clouds. Eventually a complex frontal storm develops. Winter temperatures are so mild in the Pampas that snow is rare and usually only appears as brief flurries.

Over the years, livestock grazing and the spread of crop farming have reduced the once lush native grasses of the

Argentine Pampas. Nevertheless, the Pampas region's location, mild climate, and rich soils make it one of the world's major food-producing areas. As we shall see, the Pampas are the heartland of Argentina, the source of its greatest wealth, and home of about 80 percent of its population.

THE NORTHEAST

Argentina's third major physical region is the Northeast. This lowland area lies east of the Andes, south of Paraguay, west of the Uruguay River, and north of the Pampas. It comprises three kinds of land—the Chaco, Mesopotamia, and Paraná Plateau. The Chaco is a low-lying, gently sloping alluvial plain. An alluvial plain is composed of sediments deposited by rivers. The Pilcomayo and Bermejo rivers deposit the sediments to form the plain before they join the Paraná River. The Argentine Chaco is part of a much larger plain, the Greater Chaco, which also makes up southeastern Bolivia and western Paraguay. (The word *Chaco* comes from a Quechua Indian word for a hunt in which the hunters would form a wide circle and close in on their prey. Quechua-speakers were the original inhabitants of the neighboring Andes Mountains of Bolivia and Peru.)

Mesopotamia, Greek for "land between two rivers," is the second kind of land in the Northeast. Argentina's Mesopotamia is between the Paraná and Uruguay rivers. The area is composed of broad plains that often flood during the summer.

The Paraná Plateau is the third land area of the Northeast. It is an elevated, flat surface built up by a series of ancient volcanic lava flows. The plateau stretches from southern Brazil to eastern Paraguay. The narrow Argentine province of Misiones is wedged between these two countries and is part of the plateau. Here, the Paraná River and its tributaries have cut deep canyons. Where the rivers drop over the edges of lava formations, there are spectacular falls, including Iguazú Falls on the Iguazú River. The spectacular

Iguazú Falls is one of Argentina's most spectacular sights. The waterfalls are a combination of more than 270 separate falls.

Iguazú Falls are located on the boundary between Argentina and Brazil and are an important tourist attraction for both countries. A huge hydroelectric project built jointly by the governments of Argentina, Brazil, and Paraguay harnesses the tremendous power of the Iguazú, as it thunders through narrow gorges near the falls. All three countries share electricity produced by the project.

Northeastern Argentina is close enough to the equator to have a tropical climate. Average monthly temperatures of Formosa range from 63°F (17°C) in July to 82°F (28°C) in January. Daily high temperatures can be extreme. In Rivadavia, a small town in Chaco Province, temperatures have reached 120°F (49°C). This is the highest temperature ever recorded in South America. The western Chaco receives only about 25 inches (635 millimeters) of rainfall per year. Because it is located closer to the ocean, the eastern Chaco receives up to 55 inches (1,400 millimeters) of rainfall. Virtually all of the rainfall in the Chaco is from summer thundershowers. Due to a winter drought, the natural vegetation of the Chaco has drought-tolerant scrub woodlands with patches of grassy savanna. Owners of large estates use the Chaco's savannas for cattle grazing. Quebracho, a scrawny scrub tree, dominates the woodland. Its name means "break-ax" because of its extremely hard wood. It is a source of tannin (used to tan leather), fence posts, railroad ties, and firewood.

Mesopotamia receives about 55 inches (1,400 millimeters) of rainfall per year. Summer convectional storms and weak winter cold fronts spread precipitation fairly evenly through the year. Floods are a serious natural hazard in low-lying Mesopotamia, as well as in the Pampas. Floods in both regions usually occur in late summer and fall because of heavy downpours from convective storms. Argentina's worst flood was in 1983, when raging waters left more than 5 million people homeless in Mesopotamia and adjoining areas of the Chaco and Pampas.

Natural vegetation of Mesopotamia consists of swamps on floodplains and savanna grasses with palm trees on the higher land. Soils are generally deep and fertile. Each summer, however, floods saturate the floodplain areas, making the soils there soggy and difficult to plow.

The Paraná Plateau is the country's wettest area. It receives about 70 inches (1,800 millimeters) of precipitation annually. As in Mesopotamia, summer convective storms and winter frontal storms spread the rainfall evenly throughout the year. Higher elevations here initiate additional cloud formation and rainfall. Soils of the plateau are moderately fertile and support dense mixed forests of pine and broadleaf evergreen trees. *Yerba maté*, or Paraguay tea, is a beverage made from the leaves of a tree native to the forests of this part of South America.

PATAGONIA

Patagonia is Argentina's fourth and largest major physical division. This mainly arid plateau region is larger than the state of Texas. Sailors under the command of Ferdinand Magellan gave the region its name. In 1520, on his voyage to the Pacific Ocean, Magellan stopped along Argentina's southern coast to resupply his ships with food and fresh water. His landing party noted that the native people put tufts of grass in their shoes to keep their feet warm. Because they looked so large-footed, the way a person does in snowshoes, the Spanish dubbed them "Patagones," which means "big feet." This name remains part of Argentina today!

Patagonia parallels the Andes south from the Colorado River to Tierra del Fuego. The plateau tilts downward from west to east toward the sea. It begins with average elevations of about 2,000 feet (610 meters) at the base of the Andes Mountains and ends in rugged sea cliffs at the Atlantic shore. In the past, Andean glaciers pushed onto the western edge of Patagonia and gouged out large basins there. The glaciers have melted away, but small Andean streams fill the depressions to form lakes. Lava plateaus make up much of Patagonia. Occasional tabletop mountains and small volcanic cones break the sameness of its windblown, pebble-strewn surface. The Negro, Chubut, and Santa Cruz rivers have cut deep canyons into the elevated surfaces of the region.

Patagonia's desert temperatures are cool in comparison to those of the tropical North. The difference is due largely to latitude. For example, the southern Patagonia town of Río Gallegos, which is 52 degrees south latitude, has an average annual temperature of 47°F (8°C). In contrast, Formosa, which is 26 degrees south latitude in the eastern Chaco, has an average temperature of 73°F (23°C). Moreover, the North has no plant-killing frosts, so the growing season is year round. The growing season in southern Patagonia, on the other hand, is practically non-existent. Only hardy shrubs and grasses grow there.

The towering Andes influence the climate of Patagonia in two significant ways. First, air sinks downslope from the mountains to produce dry Andean winds (*zondas*) across Patagonia's plateaus. These winds can blow continuously with gusts up to 50 miles per hour (80 kilometers per hour) for days at a time. Such wind speeds are capable of blowing an adult man off his feet! *Zondas* in the winter make Patagonia's already cool temperatures feel colder. The winds are so troublesome that many towns and ranches in the region are located in steep-walled canyons for shelter.

The second way the Andes influence the climate is by blocking moisture-bearing winds. Patagonia is located in the middle latitudes (30 degrees south to 55 degrees south). Throughout the world, prevailing westerly winds in the middle latitudes bring moist air to west coasts of continents. In Patagonia, the Andes block the moist air and force it to rise, cool, and precipitate over mountains in Chile. By the time the winds cross the Andes and descend into Argentina, they are dry. Climatologists (scientists who study climate) call Patagonia a rain shadow desert, as it is in a dry zone on the side of mountains that is sheltered from the wind. The region receives an average of only 10 inches (254 millimeters) of precipitation annually.

Sarmiento illustrates the coldness and dryness of Patagonia. This small town in the Chico River Canyon of Chubut Province holds the record for the lowest temperature in South America, a bone-chilling -17°F (-27°C). Precipitation is low, averaging just 5.5 inches (140 millimeters) each year. The dryness of Patagonia extends all the way to the eastern coast of Argentina. It is the only mid-latitude desert in the Southern Hemisphere with a coastline on the eastern side of a continent.

Desert soils, such as Patagonia's, tend to have surprisingly large amounts of calcium, potassium, and other inorganic nutrients that plants need in order to grow. The nutrients remain in the soil, however, because soil water, which is in short supply, is necessary for plants to absorb them. Only plants that need small amounts of nutrients and water are able to survive in deserts. Grasses that grow in widely spaced clumps (bunch grasses) survive best. The desert also supports a number of xerophytes (Latin for "dry plants"), such as certain small bushes, cacti, and agaves. There are hardly any trees in Patagonia. Small scattered patches of Araucaria pine and southern beech exist. They appear where openings in the Andes allow snow and rain from Pacific Ocean storms to sneak through. Because it is a cold, windswept desert and is isolated from the country's main centers of economic development, Patagonia is very sparsely settled.

WILDLIFE

Nearly all of Argentina's original wildlife has suffered from human pressures of habitat destruction and hunting. Before humans arrived in large numbers, Argentina was home to four main hoofed animals: guanacos, vicuñas, alpacas, and llamas. These grazing animals are distant relatives of the camel. Native peoples hunted all but the llama for meat, hides, and fur or wool. Europeans did the same, but their guns were more efficient in killing them. Today, few of the animals remain alive in the wild.

The guanaco is the smallest of the four animals, about the size of a small deer. Early settlers encountered thousands of guanacos roaming the Pampas, but the animals also live in the Andes and Patagonia. The vicuña, alpaca, and llama are native to the Andes. Only the vicuña remains undomesticated. Since days of the Incas, hunters have prized its fine textured wool. Unfortunately, due to overhunting, the vicuña was nearly extinct by 1960. Those that remain are in the most inaccessible parts of the Andes. Recent efforts in establishing national parks and organizations for protecting vicuñas have managed to increase the population substantially.

Alpaca and llamas are very similar in appearance and are twice the size of the guanaco and vicuña. Their habitat includes the Andes Mountains from northern Chile to southern Peru, including northwestern Argentina. The llama is the Andes' main domesticated animal. They were excellent pack animals in the rugged Andes Mountains in the days of the Inca Empire. Now ranchers raise them for their wool. Recently, there has been a resurgence of interest in using llamas as pack animals and as guards to prevent dogs and coyotes from attacking herds of sheep. The alpaca is not dependent on people for survival; therefore, it is not truly domesticated. However, local ranchers often herd them in flocks and raise them for their hides and wool.

The speedy puma (mountain lion) is the main natural predator of Argentina's hoofed animals. Pumas sneak up on prey that are grazing or sleeping. Their hunting range extends east to the dry Pampa, but it is mainly a mountain dweller. The majestic giant condor, with wingspans up to 12 feet (4 meters), makes its home in the Andes' rocky cliffs. It ranges as far south as Tierra del Fuego. Fish, such as native perch, migratory salmon, and introduced trout, swim in the lakes and rivers of both the Andes and Patagonia. Fish-eating birds, such as hawks and flamingos, seek out their meals in the same habitats.

The marshes and swamps of Mesopotamia provide one of the best areas in Argentina to observe wildlife. Marsh deer, fish-eating bats, giant anteaters, tapir (a pig-like animal), capybara (the world's largest rodent), and caiman (similar to an alligator) are common, as are many large migratory birds. The nutria, a large rodent, is the source of thousands of fur coats so popular in Argentina and Uruguay. Interestingly, the famous chinchilla—another fur-bearing animal—had its origins in highland areas of northwestern Argentina and adjacent areas. Unlike nutrias, hunters and trappers killed off most chinchillas in their original habitats by 1917. However, a California farmer took a few surviving individuals to the United States. Today, farmers in the United States raise them for their fur and for sale as pets. A coat made of wild South American chinchilla pelts can cost as much as $100,000.

The giant anteater lives in the humid forests of northern Argentina. It uses its narrow head and long tongue to reach inside anthills and termite mounds.

Argentina's small sections of forests in Mesopotamia and Paraná Plateau have a mix of wildlife. These include howler monkeys, rattlesnakes, parrots, jaguars, and ocelots living among trees and vines. Sadly, expanding human occupation and hunting threatens these creatures' habitats and the region has lost much of its native wildlife. For example, the pampas deer, once as common as the guanaco, is gone. The drier fringes still harbor a few pumas and far-ranging guanaco.

Rheas, flightless birds about the size of a turkey, used to run in huge flocks across Patagonia's plateaus. The rhea's famous gigantic cousin is the African Ostrich. Since the arrival of Europeans, rheas have all but disappeared due to overhunting and the introduction of predators, such as dogs. There are still a few wild rheas and a few are kept fenced in as farmyard pets.

Patagonia and Tierra del Fuego have marine wildlife widely distributed on their coasts, including penguins, sea lions, fur seals, elephant seals, dolphins, and whales. Several coastal reserves, from Río Negro Province southward to Tierra del Fuego, have large numbers of wild animals that are one of the greatest tourist attractions in the region.

Feral animals, or animals that were once tame but are now wild, roam remote areas of the Andes and Patagonia. Herds of wild donkeys live high up in the *altiplano* of Argentina's northern Andes. They are descendents of donkeys that carried supplies from Argentina to Spanish silver mines in Bolivia. Large herds of feral horses, whose ancestors carried Argentine soldiers and fugitive Indians into pitched battles, still hide out in Patagonia's canyons and ravines.

DINOSAURS

Argentina's most famous animals no longer exist—the dinosaurs. These huge beasts lived some 250 million to about 65 million years ago. Climate was warmer then and the Andes and the rain shadow they cast did not exist. Therefore, Argentina's climate was wetter and warmer, and dinosaurs flourished there. Paleontologists (scientists who study fossils) discovered Argentina's first dinosaur bone fossils in Argentina in 1825. Patagonia is where paleontologists have made the most recent dinosaur discoveries. The region contains one of the world's largest known treasures of dinosaur fossils.

The bipedal (two-legged) Patagonian *Gigantosaurus* is among the largest carnivorous (meat-eating) dinosaurs ever discovered. Another giant was the herbivorous (plant-eating) *Argentinosaurus.* Four pillar-like legs and a backbone five feet thick supported this heavy, 120-foot-long creature. New evidence suggests that large carnivorous dinosaurs may have formed packs, perhaps for hunting. Paleontologists usually attribute such behavior to smaller dinosaurs, such as those depicted in the movie *Jurassic Park.*

Small, scattered groups of Native Americans lived in Argentina before the arrival of Europeans. Sadly, most Indians succumbed to disease or died in battle with settlers.

Argentina
Through Time

Before the arrival of Spanish colonists in 1516 A.D., there were probably no more than 105,000 indigenous (native) people living in Argentina. Population density was generally low. In most areas, people lived by hunting wild animals and gathering edible seeds, roots, berries, and fruits. Some indigenous peoples in Argentina practiced agriculture, which provides more food than does hunting and gathering. Consequently, these groups had denser populations.

One area of high population density was in the northern forests and highlands. Here, the Guaraní people practiced slash-and-burn farming. To make space for settlements and crops, farmers would cut down trees and set fires to clear areas of plants. The ash fertilized crops, which included corn, cassava (manioc), and sweet potatoes. Settlements were small, with 50 to 100 individuals living in a community. When the land became infertile, the community moved to another unoccupied site.

Other areas of high population density were in the Northwest, in the low Andean valleys along the eastern edge of the *altiplano*, and in the Andean piedmont basins farther south. Several indigenous groups lived in this area in permanent settlements. They developed trade connections with one another. The most advanced group was the Huarpe; they lived in Cuyo, a basin and range area in the Andean piedmont. The towns of Mendoza and San Juan are located there today. Native groups of the Northwest practiced irrigated agriculture and grew corn, squash, beans, and quinoa (an Andean grain crop used in making biscuits, porridge, soups, and steamed puddings). They also herded llamas.

Small groups of nomadic peoples settled the remainder of Argentina. In addition to the bow and arrow, they used the *boleadora* (or *bola*) for hunting. The *boleadora* is a throwing weapon unique to Argentina. It consists of three ropes or straps with stones attached at each end. The hunter grasps one of the stones, whirls the other two overhead, aims at the legs of his prey, and lets go. (The prey could be a guanaco, deer, rabbit, partridge, or some other game.) The whirling straps, propelled by the weight of the stones, tangle around the legs of the animal and cause it to fall.

Nomadic groups moved in bands of 15 to 20 people. The Querandí and Puelche were two of several groups that roamed the Pampas. Araucanians lived in southern Andean passes and foothills. Even fewer Indians lived in the harsh Patagonian desert. As nomads, these groups did not remain in one place long enough to grow crops. They relied mainly on hunting and gathering.

Spanish policy was to control the more densely settled northern areas. Colonists needed native people for labor. However, the native population declined drastically for four reasons. First, the Spaniards killed natives who resisted their control. Firearms and horses gave the Spaniards military superiority. Second, the Spaniards enslaved many of the indigenous people who survived the massacres. Enslaved Indians worked in mines, grew crops, and raised livestock used by the Spaniards. Unfortunately, slaves received little food or rest. Many died of malnutrition and exhaustion. Third, many native people died of diseases introduced by the Spaniards. The Europeans were resistant to the germs, but native people were not. Deadly epidemics of influenza, smallpox, typhus, and other diseases spread rapidly among them. Finally, the Indians lost their will to live. Their families and relatives were dying, communities were breaking up, and cultures were disappearing. Many troubled adults committed suicide. More and more women stopped having babies and, if born, mothers often killed their babies to save them from disease and starvation.

Indigenous peoples barely survived after Argentina became independent from Spanish colonial rule. Independence brought more foreign settlers and the gradual settlement of the Pampas. Some native people survived in rural areas by marrying European settlers. Others survived by fleeing to remote areas. The Tehuelches fled the Pampas to southern Patagonia. Araucanians had already been living on the western edge of Patagonia, just north of the Negro River. They had spread into this region from southern Chile in the 16th century. The Araucanians had a reputation as fierce warriors. Before Spaniards arrived in southern Chile, they had battled against the Inca army and stopped the Incas from spreading into that region.

The Tehuelches and Araucanians began acquiring horses from the Spanish in the 1600s. Horses, grazing on open grasslands, were easy to steal from the Spaniards. There were no fences in those days. Possession of horses radically changed the Tehuelche and Araucanian cultures. Both groups became excellent horsemen and the fleet-footed horse expanded the distance they could travel from their villages to hunt. Moreover, horses made it easier for nomadic bands to conduct raids against their European enemies. These horseback-riding hunters and warriors remained free until the late 1800s.

EARLY SPANISH SETTLEMENT

Spain became interested in what is now Argentina in 1516. Juan Díaz de Solís led a Spanish expedition of three ships southward along South America's Atlantic coast. He was looking for a pathway to the Pacific Ocean and the profitable Asian trade that lay beyond. After passing the coast of Portuguese Brazil, he saw the immense opening of an estuary. (A later explorer, believing that the estuary led to silver-rich areas, named it the *Río de la Plata*, or "River of Silver.") Thinking this might be the shortcut to the Pacific Ocean, Solís diverted his ships into the estuary and claimed the region for the Spanish Empire. A short time later, a small band of warriors captured and killed Solís and most of his crew. Thus, the expedition ended in disaster.

This event did not end Spanish interest in the area. In 1532, Francisco Pizarro landed an expeditionary force on the coast of Peru. From there, he led a lightning-fast conquest of the Inca Empire. This victory made the Río de la Plata estuary strategically important. It was the entry point to unexplored land that separated Spain's recently acquired gold- and silver-rich Andean possessions from Portuguese Brazil.

This interior area makes up what is now northern Argentina and Paraguay. Neither the Spanish nor the Portuguese knew what resources the region held. The Spanish moved quickly to explore and settle the area. They approached from two directions: the Río de la Plata and Peru (the heartland of the former Inca Empire). The Spanish Crown gave Pedro de Mendoza permission to lead an expeditionary force from Spain to Argentina. Mendoza sailed into the Río de la Plata estuary in 1536 with 1,500 men and established the settlement of Buenos Aires. The Querandí laid siege to the settlement, however, and

Some of the first European settlements in Argentina were missions built by Jesuit missionaries. The ruins of a Jesuit mission still stand in San Ignacio, a town in the northeastern part of the country.

the setters abandoned it in 1537. Mendoza and most of his men eventually left Buenos Aires to return to Spain.

In spite of many hardships, a small group of Spanish settlers remained in South America. They left Buenos Aires and traveled north, up the Paraná and Paraguay Rivers. There, with the help of friendly Guaraní Indians, they founded the city of Asunción (now the capital of Paraguay). The area soon became the focus of Jesuit missionaries and Spanish settlement. For a time, the Guaraní people became pawns in the struggle for control of the region between missionaries and Spanish and Portuguese colonial administrators. *The Mission*, a movie starring Robert De Niro, describes the true story of a Spanish soldier and a Jesuit priest who united to save a mission in this region. Ultimately, the Spaniards organized the native peoples to produce exports for Buenos Aires. They grew cotton, made cloth, and produced *yerba maté*, a tea that became a popular drink among the colonists and eventually modern-day Argentines.

Many early Spanish settlers in northern Argentina came from Peru. Spaniards conquered native settlements in the valleys bordering the *altiplano* and basins of the Andean piedmont. By the end of the 16th century, a string of towns extended from Salta to Tucumán and Córdoba. The conquerors enslaved the native peoples, forcing them to harvest crops and raise cattle and mules. The Spaniards also forced the enslaved people to grow cotton and produce cotton goods.

RISE OF BUENOS AIRES AND REGIONAL CONFLICTS

The Portuguese established a trading post on the northern coast of the Rio de la Plata in what is now Uruguay. In order to keep up with the Portuguese, Spaniards from Asunción re-established the settlement of Buenos Aires in 1580. A favorable location for smuggling led to the town's rise in prominence. Spanish colonies, such as Argentina, were supposed to supply money and goods to help pay for the costs of governing Spain. The Crown forced its colonies to pay taxes on all traded goods. Moreover, it ruled that colonies could only trade with Spain. Argentina was no exception to these policies. Spain demanded that all imported and exported goods go through faraway Lima, so that it could control Argentina's trade and collect taxes. Shipments to or from Lima, however, required crossing the Andes, making the goods very expensive. Price inflation forced most Argentine merchants to purchase and sell goods through Portuguese smugglers in the port of Buenos Aires. Smugglers and merchants could exchange goods at lower prices, because they did not include Andean transport costs and Crown taxes.

In the 18th century, the Spanish throne came under control of a new ruling family—the Bourbons. The Bourbons recognized the need for economic reforms. They saw that they were losing tax revenue because of smuggling in Buenos Aires. They also recognized the economic potential and strategic importance of the Río de la Plata region. In 1776, the Bourbons created the Viceroyalty of Río La Plata with Buenos Aires as its capital. This large colony consisted of what today are Argentina, Paraguay, Uruguay, and southern Bolivia. The action created a local government that could collect taxes. Additionally, the Crown made Buenos Aires a free Port of Spain in 1778. This action meant that Argentina could bypass Lima and trade directly with Spain. Consequently, a cattle industry in the Pampas expanded rapidly. Hides, leather products, tallow, and salted beef were the main products. Additionally, silver from Bolivia passed through Buenos Aires.

Buenos Aires boomed as trade flourished. Residents referred to themselves with pride as *porteños* (people of the port), and still do so today. Growing industries needed more labor. The trade in slaves from Portuguese colonies in Africa increased. So did immigration of laborers from Spain. By 1800, Buenos Aires had become the major urban market, the heart of the cattle economy, the financial capital, and the cultural center of Argentina. The interior cities, led by Córdoba, Santa Fe, and Rosario, were bitter that they did not receive what they thought was their full share. Spain was satisfied though. As legal trading increased, so did its share of the tax revenues that trading generated.

Buenos Aires prospered under the new Spanish policies. However, the *porteños* were not content to remain a Spanish colony. American colonies' independence from Great Britain and the French Revolution's spirit of equality caused many Argentines to question the right of Spain to control their affairs. Moreover, events in Europe were weakening Spain's control of Argentina and its other colonies.

In 1806 and 1807, the British attempted to seize Buenos Aires to establish a base in the region. The colonists, however, successfully fought off the invaders. Their success at defending themselves increased the colonists' confidence that they could survive and prosper without Spain's help. When the French invaded Spain in 1810, the Argentines took advantage of Spain's weakness and began to run their own affairs. In Buenos Aires, a council of 200 *porteños* organized their own independent government to administer the Viceroyalty of Río de la Plata. The areas outside La Plata, however, opposed this action. By 1816, powerful military strongmen (*caudillos*) had divided Argentina into separate territories. The *caudillos* lacked the qualities to lead an entire nation. They were usually illiterate bullies who led undisciplined, murderous armies. Their troops were skilled horsemen and experts with the lasso, *boleadora*, and knife. The *caudillos* used their armies to kill or severely punish anyone who questioned their authority to rule. They were uninterested in the greater cause of nation building.

STRUGGLE FOR ORDER AND STABILITY

Argentina formally declared independence from Spain on July 9, 1816. From 1816 to 1829, Argentina was turbulent. *Caudillos* were engaged in warfare among themselves. No one could agree on a constitution that was acceptable to all political and regional factions.

Much of the chaos resulted from the lack of a leader who could unite Argentina. There was one missed opportunity. In 1812, José de San Martín, who was to become one of the Argentina's most famous heroes and one of the great liberators of South America, arrived in Argentina from Spain. He was born in 1788 in the Viceroyalty of Río de la Plata. When he was eight years old, he went with his family to Spain, where he later became an army officer. When Napoleon defeated the Spanish, San Martín offered his services in Argentina. There, he organized an army to help gain independence. After winning a

José de San Martín helped liberate much of South America from Spanish rule. He is one of Argentina's greatest national heroes.

crucial battle against Spanish loyalists, the Buenos Aires government made San Martín head of the Northern Army and he set up his headquarters in Mendoza. It was here that he conceived his plan to march his army across the Andes and free Chile and Peru from Spanish rule.

In 1817, after defeating the Spanish in most of Argentina, San Martín led his army into central Chile, where he surprised and routed the Spaniards. He then joined forces with Chilean army rebels and advanced northward to capture Lima.

Eventually his troops helped Símon Bolívar, the great Venezuelan general, gain victory over the Spanish in Ecuador. Unfortunately, San Martín did not return to Argentina. Although his country desperately needed a strong hero to rally around, he sailed to France. Despite his untimely departure, Argentines still respect San Martín as the hero of their national independence.

While San Martín was liberating Chile and Peru, petty feuds among rival *caudillos* boiled over into renewed warfare. In Argentina, the two main political parties had opposite views about how to run the new nation. Buenos Aires became the home of the Unitarist Party, which wanted a strong central government in which the capital city regulated trade with outlying regions. In the outlying areas, the Federalist Party was dominant. Composed mostly of cattlemen, the Federalists sought limitations on the power of merchants in Buenos Aires. They wanted to give more power to the country's outlying regions. The disagreement between Buenos Aires and interior rural regions spilled over into civil warfare. Federalists, backed by *caudillo* militias from outlying provinces, fought against the Unitarists and the *caudillo* of Buenos Aires. Control of the government changed between the Unitarists and Federalists several times. The fighting halted Argentine trade and economic life. In the absence of a strong leader, Argentina seemed destined to split into separate countries.

JUAN MANUEL DE ROSAS

Amid this conflict, arose Juan Manuel de Rosas, the *caudillo* of Buenos Aires. He was the first leader to govern independent Argentina with unquestioned authority. Rosas ruled Argentina longer than any other leader, from 1829–1852. He was different from most other *caudillos,* because he could read and write. His literacy enabled him to distribute declarations of policy and to organize a strong army. Rosas united Argentina under a strong central government with Buenos Aires as its capital. He required that all goods be imported and exported through Buenos Aires. Taxes on these goods brought money to the capital. To calm the Federalists, who opposed taxes that benefited merchants in Buenos Aires, Rosas did nothing to develop international trade that would benefit the capital and main seaport. Additionally, he allowed *caudillos* to remain in control of their territories. Rosas himself remained the *caudillo* of Buenos Aires, and he installed *caudillos* who supported him as heads of other provinces. Each *caudillo* could maintain an army. Rosas also permitted each *caudillo* to levy his own taxes and to keep the income for his province.

Rosas brought control to the government, but Argentines paid for it with their freedom. He was a dictator who created the *Mazorca*, a secret police force. It spied on, harassed, and punished people who disobeyed his rules. Rosas was so powerful and ruthless that he made everyone in Buenos Aires wear a red scarf, a pin with his portrait, and a ribbon saying "Death to the Savage Unitarians!" Everyone obeyed, as people knew that the *Mazorca* sometimes slit the throats of Rosas' opponents. Many Unitarians fled Argentina to Uruguay and Brazil during Rosas' reign. Not surprisingly, Rosas' brutality made him an unpopular ruler, even among Federalists. In 1852, Argentines overthrew his government and forced him to leave the country.

FOUNDATIONS OF THE MODERN STATE

With Rosas' overthrow, a new era of political and economic development began for Argentina. In 1853, Argentines met in Santa Fe to write a constitution. (Although suspended on several occasions by military juntas, it survives in modified form today.) The *porteños* of Buenos Aires, however, refused to become part of the country. They established their own independent state and fought a civil war against the other provinces. Finally, in 1862, Buenos Aires agreed to become a part of Argentina, but on its own terms.

From 1862 until 1930, Argentina enjoyed a period of political stability that encouraged territorial and technological growth. European investments, especially British money, built railroads and telegraph lines. Stability and economic growth also attracted European immigrants, particularly Italians who became a reliable source of labor for the busy farms of the Pampas. Even Welsh immigrants were enticed to settle in Patagonia's remote river valleys. Public education also spread throughout Argentina.

Argentina's growing population included a middle class of merchants, artisans, government employees, factory managers, farmers, and businesspeople. The middle class evolved from the tremendous economic growth that took place between 1880 and 1910. During this period of "Golden Years," Buenos Aires' economy boomed. Its population nearly doubled in the 1880s.

The economy also boomed in the countryside. Remaining indigenous peoples were defeated and scattered, making room for more European settlers. Large ranches bred and raised cattle that produced "more pounds on the hoof" than the scrawny, half-wild cattle they raised before. Cattlemen were getting a better price for beef, as the development of refrigeration enabled them to export fresh meat to European markets. (In earlier years, cattlemen had salted beef to preserve it.) Argentines also sold leather goods and wheat to Europe. Italians and Basques established sheep ranches on the Pampas and produced wool for England's textile mills. Swiss, German, Italian, and French immigrants started small farms in Buenos Aires and several other provinces.

THE GREAT DEPRESSION AND WORLD WAR II

Argentina's "Golden Years" ended in the 1930s, when the impact of the Great Depression reached the country. This economic depression brought a sharp, worldwide downturn in industry, commerce, and employment. The Great Depression badly damaged Argentina's economy. In the chaos, a military dictatorship took control of the country. Some Argentine industries began to produce goods that previously were imported. These industries provided jobs for thousands of unemployed rural poor who moved into the cities. Growth of a poor urban worker class later played a prominent role in the rise of Juan Domingo Perón. The economic crisis continued into World War II, because the fighting made international trade nearly impossible.

World War II sharply divided Argentina. Large numbers of Argentines of Italian and German background sympathized with the Axis powers—Germany, Italy, and Japan. These sympathizers wanted Argentina to maintain diplomatic relations with the Axis countries. Many other Argentines disliked the Axis governments. They valued Argentina's economic ties with the Allies—the United States, Great Britain, France, and others—and wanted Argentina to side with them. Street demonstrations erupted, pitting the two sides against one another. Although most other nations of the Western Hemisphere sided with the Allies, the Argentine government declared itself neutral. It was not until 1945, at the end of the war, that Argentina declared war on the Axis powers.

JUAN DOMINGO PERÓN

Juan Domingo Perón, an army colonel, rose to power after the Argentine military overthrew the government in 1943. The military leaders appointed Perón secretary of labor and social welfare. He won the support of the working people by increasing pay, pensions, and other benefits. Previous governments had ignored these laborers. Largely through their support, Perón won the presidency in 1946. Soon after, his supporters formed the Justicialist party, which Argentines popularly call the Perónist party. This party has influenced Argentine politics ever since. Perón helped form powerful workers' unions. During his first term as president, Perón used his political and economic influence to raise the proportion of union workers from about 10 to 70 percent.

President Juan Domingo Perón was one of the most popular leaders in Argentine history. His beautiful wife Eva, better known as "Evita," gained the love of the people by championing the rights of women, workers, and the poor.

Perón's second wife, Eva Duarte de Perón, gave him good political advice. Her popularity greatly strengthened his political support. She gave impassioned speeches to rally her husband's supporters. She also helped him organize the labor movement. Moreover, she mobilized women and won them the right to vote in 1947. Workers and women admired Mrs. Perón for her efforts to organize charities to help disadvantaged people. They referred to her affectionately as "Evita."

Perón increased governmental spending on transportation, public works, and housing for workers. However, these programs were so costly that he was forced to borrow huge sums of money to pay for them. He also allowed the country's agricultural economy to decline. Perón also began assuming more power and making decisions without consulting other government officials. He even began censoring newspapers. Despite rapidly growing public displeasure against his administration, Perón changed the Argentine constitution to increase his power and allow him to run for a second term.

Perón's popularity declined rapidly soon after his reelection in 1952. Unfortunately, "Evita" died of cancer at age 33, shortly after his second term began. However, her political shrewdness and popularity probably would not have saved his presidency. The country was almost bankrupt. Perón had angered almost everyone: journalists, large landowners, small farmers, business people, and even many urban workers. He also lost the support of the Roman Catholic Church by limiting its authority. Finally, in 1955, the military overthrew Perón. He fled to Spain to live in exile until 1975, when a desperate Argentina asked Perón to return to serve again as president.

UNSTABLE POLITICAL CLIMATE

The governments that followed Perón faced increasing social unrest. Living costs soared. There were riots, revolts, strikes, and bombings. Government secret police arrested, tortured, and murdered opposition members, who were mainly Perónist politicians, union leaders, and student activists. In response, extremists kidnapped and assassinated conservative politicians, judges, and journalists. Argentine governments shifted between civilian presidents and military dictators.

In 1973, army leaders allowed a Perónist leader named Héctor José Cámpora to become president. They hoped he could reestablish order. Later that year, Perón returned from Spain. Cámpora resigned and Argentines reelected the aging Perón, who died in office in mid-1974. His third wife, Isabel, who had held the vice presidency, replaced him. She became the Western Hemisphere's first woman president.

Unfortunately, she was unqualified to run the country. Argentina's economy was in shambles. Inflation was running 400 percent, meaning the price of goods were four times higher than during the previous year. Moreover, terrorist organizations representing both radicals and conservatives continued to kill one another and innocent bystanders. These were bloody times that would severely challenge even the most experienced politician.

In 1976, military leaders arrested Isabel Perón and took over the government. At first, many Argentines celebrated. However, the bloodshed increased as the military carried out "The Dirty War" (1976–1983). In this war, the military used secret police and other right-wing groups to kidnap, torture, and execute as many as 9,000 civilians. No one knows the exact number. Some of these people may have participated in terrorist acts. But the government never charged any of them with crimes or allowed them a public trial. To this day, authorities have found the bodies of only a few of the missing civilians. Argentines call them *los desaparecidos* (the disappeared).

A member of the military junta, General Leopoldo Galtieri, became president in 1982. Galtieri attempted to direct Argentines' attention away from their country's problems by invading the Falkland Islands in 1982. These islands, claimed by both the United Kingdom and Argentina, are located about 300 miles (480 kilometers) off the Argentine coast. Great Britain had occupied this tiny outpost, where sheep far outnumber people, since 1833. Galtieri and his advisors did not believe the British would send troops to stop the invasion of a small and remote group of islands. A successful invasion, the junta reasoned, would rally Argentines behind their faltering government. To their surprise, Great Britain responded with a powerful force of navy ships, planes, and marines. In only 74 days, the poorly trained Argentines surrendered to the British. After nationwide protests against the war, humiliated military leaders returned the government to civilian rule in 1983.

RECENT DEVELOPMENTS

Argentina emerged from the Falklands War in desperate condition. Political unrest had discouraged most of Argentina's European investors and markets. By 1983, its foreign debt had grown to $50 billion and its annual inflation rate was 137 percent. Moreover, a history of political corruption, military coups, and the foolhardy Falklands War made Argentines distrustful of government.

There have been encouraging signs since 1983. Each positive development, however, has a negative side. Democracy has returned, but corruption and regional divisions still hamper presidential administrations. The country has wealth, but nearly all of it is in the hands of about 1 percent of the people. Inflation has decreased to less than 10 percent, but the national debt is sky high. In other words, Argentina's history has created great political and economic difficulties. These problems persist today and have no simple solutions. Argentines are among the most diverse and best-educated people in South America. Perhaps they will eventually find the needed solutions.

The majority of Argentines are Catholic. Each year, believers take part in a pilgrimage to San Cayetano Church in Buenos Aires.

4

People
and Culture

Argentines cannot decide if they are Latin Americans or Europeans. It has been said that an Argentine is a Spaniard who speaks like an Italian, dresses like a Frenchman, and thinks he is British.

(Foster, et al., *Culture and Customs of Argentina*)

IDENTITY, IMAGE AND OPINIONS

Argentines are among the world's most interesting people because they are so complex. Their culture is a blend of several European cultures. Yet unlike culturally diverse North Americans, they are unsure of who they really are. Scholars do not fully understand why Argentines have this identity crisis. A deep concern for understanding one's self appears to be part of the Argentine culture. There are a surprising number of psychiatrists and psychologists in Buenos Aires. A majority of this city's middle class adults have undergone psychoanalysis!

A connection may exist between Argentines' uncertainty about who they are and the importance that they place on physical appearance. Buenos Aires supposedly has more residents who have undergone plastic surgery than any other city in the world! Argentines have a reputation for meticulous grooming and placing a high value on style and quality of clothing. They dress up on weekends, when going out for dinner, and for many other occasions. The wealthy class of Buenos Aires is most influential in image-conscious Argentina. David J. Keeling, author of *Buenos Aires: Global Dreams, Local Crises*, describes this influence when he states, "tuxedoed men and suntanned women in fur coats alighting from limousines and taxis, set the standards of urban fashion, taste, and elegance."

Argentines might be uncertain about who they are, or overly concerned about how they appear, but they have strong opinions about many things. They care deeply about family, music, art, literature, and politics. Generally, once you get to know Argentines, they do not hesitate to express their views. Passionate discussions about various topics take place in coffeehouses, cafes, plazas, and on street corners. These discussions are usually not mere chatter, as most middle-class Argentine people are well educated, well read, and confident about most things. Many Argentine intellectuals have been educated in Europe, particularly Paris. Historically, Buenos Aires copied European trends in culture. It is Argentina's most influential city and the intellectual center of South America.

POPULATION

Argentines' uncertain self-identity may be the result of their diverse ancestry. Of the country's approximately 38 million people, about 95 percent are of assorted European ancestry. Most Argentines have Spanish or Italian backgrounds. Many early immigrants also came from Great Britain, France, and

Germany. The most striking aspect of Argentina's population is its concentration in the Pampas region. More than one-third of the people live there. Most of them reside in Buenos Aires and its suburbs. Greater Buenos Aires has more than 13 million people. Another one-third of the population is concentrated along the river network that extends north and northwest of Buenos Aires. This leaves barely 10 million people scattered throughout country's remaining vast area.

Argentina is one of the most urbanized countries in the world. About 90 percent of the population lives in cities. Greater Buenos Aires and Rio de Janeiro, Brazil, tie for the third-largest urban agglomeration in Latin America (after Mexico City and São Paulo, Brazil). The name Buenos Aires is confusing in the same way New York is: it is the name of both a province and a city. Its population is slightly over 3,000,000 persons. With a density of nearly 40,000 persons per square mile (15,000 per square kilometer), Buenos Aires is one of the most densely populated cities in Latin America. Córdoba (1,300,000 persons) is Argentina's second-largest city. Other major urban areas include: Rosario (980,000), Mar del Plata (569,000), Tucumán (532,000), Salta (486,500), and Santa Fe (450,000). Nearly all these cities are centers of provincial government. As in most countries, provincial or state capitals became the focus of population, local wealth, and power. Mar del Plata, a seaside resort and port, is the only city in this group that is not a provincial capital. Buenos Aires grew to dominate the country's people and culture due largely to its favorable location for global trade.

PORTEÑOS VERSUS PEOPLE OF THE INTERIOR

Most Argentines divide the country's people into two groups: *porteños* and people of the interior. *Porteños* live in Greater Buenos Aires. People of the interior live in the rest of the country. The authors of *Culture and Customs of Argentina* describe how these two groups disapprove of each other.

According to the authors, *porteños* regard people of the interior as being "unworldly, ugly, superstitious, and ignorant," whereas, *porteños* see themselves as "attractive, sophisticated, glamorous, and cultured." In contrast, people of the interior regard *porteños* as "aggressive, pretentious, high-strung, and loud," while they view themselves as being "humble, filled with common sense, and more down-to-earth." One might think that the negative views that each group has for the other would pull the country apart. However, like two squabbling siblings, *porteños* and people of the interior share the same history, cultural symbols, language, religion, music, art, and literature. These and other common elements of culture manage to unite Argentines.

THE GAUCHO

The free-spirited male *gaucho* is one of Argentina's most important shared symbols of culture. The *gaucho*, or Argentine cowboy, symbolizes individuality and independence. This partly real and partly legendary figure was born in the open spaces of Pampas. The earliest *gauchos* were mostly *mestizos*—people of mixed European and Indian ancestry. Some also had African parentage, a legacy of Argentina's slave trade. During the 1600s and 1700s, the *gaucho* and his descendants gradually populated the Pampas. There, they hunted wild cattle for their meat and hides and forced hostile Indians to abandon the land.

In the late 1700s, the Spanish Crown began giving large land grants to powerful men from Buenos Aires. These new landowners were military strongmen (*caudillos*). They divided their land grants into large cattle estates. They then hired *gauchos*, who were expert horsemen, to herd cattle and serve as ranch hands. The *caudillos* also used the *gauchos* as soldiers in their private armies. It was in this latter role that *gauchos* became legendary. Argentine poets, painters, songwriters, and short story authors made them fabled heroes of the war of independence against Spain. Argentines still revere the *gaucho's* way of life and his legendary past.

Argentine cowboys, called *gauchos*, participate in a competition where they trap a cow between their horses and force the animal into a corral.

The actual life of a fast-riding, fast-living *gaucho* has long vanished. A few cowboys still exist, and both Argentines and tourists like to think of them as being authentic *gauchos*. Their garb is similar to that of the *gaucho*, and their lifestyle is similar to their forbearers. In small towns outside Buenos Aires province, it is possible to see cowboys gather for a drink in local bars. They do the chores of ranch-hands, mending fences, branding cattle, breaking wild horses, and so on. They drive pickup trucks, but pride themselves in owning a horse, saddle, poncho, and knife. They also compete in rodeos, a time-honored tradition of *gauchos* and American cowboys alike, in order to display their skill with lasso and horse.

EUROPEAN IMMIGRANTS

Non-Spanish European immigrants have added to the rich ethnic makeup of Argentina's cultural heritage. Most immigration occurred between 1880 and 1930, with a second surge coming during and after World War II. The proportion of foreign-born Argentines peaked at 30 percent in 1944. Spaniards and Italians were the largest groups of immigrants during this period. Today, the Italian influence is so strong in Buenos Aires that Italian surnames outnumber Spanish. Nonetheless, Italians have not formed unique ethnic communities as they have done in New York and several other large U.S. cities.

Basques (from northeastern Spain), Welsh (from Wales in Great Britain), English, Ukrainians, Poles, and immigrants of other countries also flooded into Argentina during the late 1800s and early 1900s. Many of the early immigrants found jobs in rural towns, on cattle ranches, or on wheat and alfalfa farms. High birth rates and low death rates added to rapid population growth after World War II. Increasingly, immigrants sought jobs in large cities, as industrialization grew during and after the war. By the mid-1950s, more Argentines lived in cities than in rural areas for the first time.

European migration is the basis of today's ethnic diversity. Not all immigrants fully accepted Argentine culture. Some Argentines of British heritage retain a distinct cultural identity. About 22,000 persons of this group are scattered about the country. Roughly 25,000 Welsh-Argentines live in agricultural settlements in Chubut province. They have a separate way of life, although few still speak the Welsh language. There are other European settlements that have preserved their ethnic past, too. For example, Germans founded Eldorado in Misiones province and Villa General Belgrano in Cordoba province. Bulgarians and Slovenes settled Roque Sáenz Peña in the Chaco. Ukrainians established settlements in La Pampa province. Mountain villages in the Andean Lake District are a microcosm of Central European influence, including Swiss, German, and northern Italian. There are also groups of Russians, Austrians, Slovaks, Danes, and Norwegians in Argentina.

A common ethnic term in Spanish-speaking Latin American countries is *criollo* (Creole). In colonial days, South American-born people of pure Spanish ancestry called themselves *criollos*. They considered themselves separate from colonialists of mixed parentage. As more Spanish and other Europeans flooded into Argentina, intermarriage blurred ethnic lines. As a result, a *criollo* today is any Argentine who lives in the countryside, or in a small rural town.

OTHER ETHNIC GROUPS

A half-million Jewish people live in Argentina. From the late 1880s to 1914, tens of thousands of Jewish families came to the country. Most of them came from Russia and Eastern Europe to escape religious persecution. Some became farmers in closely-knit colonies in Entre Río and Santa Fe provinces. Most settled in Buenos Aires and worked as tailors, carpenters, saddlers, black-smiths, locksmiths, watchmakers, soap manufacturers, or house-painters. Many Jews were merchants and peddlers of clothing and secondhand merchandise. Buenos Aires is the main center of the Jewish community today. By far the largest Jewish community in Latin America, it is also the second largest in the Americas (following New York). In Buenos Aires, the Jewish community has been the target of several terrorist bomb attacks. The Israeli embassy was bombed in 1992. Two years later, a terrorist bomb killed 87 people and destroyed the city's Jewish cultural center.

Arabs and Asians add to Argentina's diverse population. There are about 1 million people of Arab descent. About 700,000 of these people are Lebanese Christians. Argentines generally respect fellow citizens regardless of their place of origin. Ancestors of former president Carlos Menem, for example, came from Syria. There are also substantial numbers of Japanese, Koreans, and Chinese residing in the country.

An estimated 1,500,000 descendants of indigenous peoples also live in Argentina. The largest group is the Quechua, who number about 915,000. Quechua was the most common language spoken in the Incan Empire. Most of the people in the Argentine Andes, in the country's far northwestern corner, speak it today. Many Quechua, about 500,000, have emigrated from northwestern and northern Argentina into slums of Buenos Aires to work on docks. The second-largest indigenous group is the Mapuche. This group descends from Araucanian warriors who fiercely resisted the tide of Argentine settlers until the 1880s. The Mapuche group is concentrated in northern Patagonia, although many Mapuche are dispersed in Buenos Aires and La Pampa provinces. The third-largest indigenous group is the Guaraní. In Paraguay, Guaraní is the official language and many Guaraní speakers in Argentina are emigrants from that country. In Argentina, most of this group is concentrated in Jujay and Salta provinces.

Most African-Argentines are the mixed descendants of slaves. Enslaved Africans worked in the mines of the Spanish Viceroyalty of the Río de la Plata. After emancipation in the 19th century, they became soldiers, *gauchos*, and general laborers in larger provincial towns. Some scholars estimate that people of African descent made up about 30 percent of the population of Buenos Aires, Tucmán, Córdoba, and Mendoza in 1810. By the late 1800s however, wars, intermarriage, and disease had decimated the country's African population. Today, the number of blacks in Argentina is very small.

Since the 1970s, most of Argentina's immigrants have arrived from neighboring countries—Bolivia, Chile, Uruguay, Peru, and Paraguay—for political or economic reasons. They work and live permanently in Argentina as agricultural or construction workers. In 2003, most of these immigrants were illegal aliens. Many Argentines blame these non-citizen workers for the economic slowdown. In reality, they take jobs few Argentines would choose to fill. In the near future, the South

American trading bloc, of which Argentina is a member, plans to grant such emigrant workers citizenship in the countries were they live.

LANGUAGE

Spanish is the official language of Argentina and is spoken by virtually everyone. In fact, Argentina has the world's fourth-largest Spanish-speaking population. (Mexico is first, followed by Colombia and Spain.) Many Argentines speak other languages, too. English is widely regarded as a required language and is taught in many primary schools. In secondary schools, most students continue to study a second language—usually English or French. In recent years, more students have begun to study Portuguese, because Portuguese-speaking Brazil is Argentina's main trading partner. Multilingualism (the ability to speak more than one language) is most common in Buenos Aires where non-Spanish newspapers are in high demand.

Argentina also has more than 20 indigenous languages. Some of these languages are spoken by no more than a dozen people. As previously noted, the numbers of Quechua, Mapuche, and Guaraní speakers are much larger. Many languages died out soon after the arrival of the Europeans. However, the languages of the Puelche of the Pampas, Ona of Tierra del Fuego, and Chané of Salta only became extinct in the last few decades. Still other indigenous languages are barely hanging on. For example, the Tehuelche tribe, which fought heroically to keep its land, is almost extinct.

Linguists (scholars who study languages) call Argentine Spanish *castellano*, because it has a strong Italian accent. Italian is also the most common second language. *Lunfardo* is a slang that residents of Buenos Aires also use. In Buenos Aires, recent immigrants who had no common language shared *lunfardo*. Slang evolves over time. Today, *lunfardo* is no longer so necessary, but it is still an important part of the city's culture. It consists mostly of informal Spanish phrases. For example, *Diez puntos* in traditional Spanish means 'ten points,' but in *lunfardo*, it means 'okay, cool, great, or fine.' *Poner las pilas* in Spanish means 'to put in the batteries,' but in *lunfardo*, it means 'to get energized.'

RELIGION

Freedom of religion is guaranteed by Argentina's constitution. The legal system, however, promotes the Roman Catholic Church. For example, a law requires parents to give their children a Christian (Catholic) name at birth. Until recently, the Catholic Church was the official state religion. As such, the Church received payments from the government and therefore played a role in the country's politics. More than 90 percent of the Argentine population is Roman Catholic, although fewer than 20 percent actively practice their religion. Protestants make up about 2 percent of the population. Another 2 percent of Argentines are Jewish.

Generally, religion plays a greater role in the lives of rural people. In rural areas, religion is quite important. People make pilgrimages to local shrines and give offerings to unofficial saints. Although many *porteños* do not attend church regularly, they show their spiritualism in less obvious ways. They make the sign of the cross on themselves when passing a church, for example. *Porteños* also show a profound reverence for the dead. They honor national heroes, such as José San Martín, Juan and Evita Perón, and Carlos Gardel (a famous singer) on the anniversary of their death. *Porteños* show their greatest reverence twice a year, in May and October, when about 5 million people participate in a 45-mile (65-kilometer) pilgrimage. They walk from downtown Buenos Aires to a basilica dedicated to the Virgin Mary in Luján.

In recent years, the Church has lost some of its influence among *porteños* and even people of the interior. The legal system no longer requires that the country's president be Catholic. Moreover, it is no longer illegal to get a divorce. The Church lost the support of many people during the late 1970s and early

The tango evolved in the slums of Buenos Aires. Today, many Argentine restaurants hold nightly tango shows for tourists.

1980s. Church leaders at that time continued to support the military government, even as evidence showed it was persecuting, kidnapping, and torturing religious workers. Many Argentine Catholics question their faith because of this sad episode.

MUSIC AND PAINTING

The most important components of traditional Argentine music are *gaucho* folk songs and the tango. Native American, European, and African traditions have all had an influence on Argentine music, too. The tango is Argentina's most famous contribution to modern music. A combination of sensual music, dance, and song, it started in smoky brothels of Buenos Aires. Its vulgar aspects disappeared as it spread into the fresh-air patios of the Buenos Aires middle class and eventually to Paris. From there, the tango became a favorite ballroom dance throughout much of the world.

Like much of Argentine culture, paintings express a mixture of European influence and *porteño* and *criollo* originality. Prilidiano Pueyrredón (1823–1870) is famous for depicting *gaucho* themes and scenes of town life in the 19th century. Another painter from that century was Cándido López (1840–1902). A former military officer, he lost his right hand in the war against Paraguay. Yet, he was still able to paint dozens of vivid scenes of the conflict. Famous painters of the 20th and early 21st centuries include Víctor Hugo Quiroga, painter of changing *criollo* life; Benito Quinquela Martín, painter of port life in Buenos Aires; Molino Campos, painter of *gauchos* and country folk; and Raúl Soldi, painter of 'dreamscapes.'

THEATER AND MOVIES

Buenos Aires is famous for its theater performances, which rival those of New York City, London, and Paris. Indeed, in the early 20th century, European theatergoers called the city the "Paris of Latin America." The name still applies today. Theater-going is most popular during the winter months (June through August). Argentina's best-known opera house is the superb Colón Theater in Buenos Aires. Modeled after the Paris Opera House, the structure occupies an entire block. The quality of its acoustics has drawn the world's finest opera singers, including Luciano Pavarotti, Julio Bocca, Maria Callas, Placido Domingo, and Arturo Toscanini.

Movies are also a popular pastime throughout Argentina. Buenos Aires alone has more than 250 movie theaters showing Argentine and international films. Argentine film directors have gained praise the world over. Several movies have earned nominations or won Oscars for best foreign film. Argentine composer Lalo Schifrin wrote themes and soundtracks for *Mission Impossible, Rush Hour, Cool Hand Luke, Dirty Harry*, and other famous U.S. movies. Argentine films in Spanish with English subtitles are available in large U.S. video stores.

LITERATURE

During the Spanish Civil War in the 1930s, many Spanish publishers moved to Buenos Aires to escape the fighting. Several remained in Argentina after the war ended. In fact, for many years Buenos Aires surpassed Madrid and Barcelona in the number of books published.

Much early Argentine literature focused on the *gaucho*. In particular, the 1870s and 1880s produced prose and poetry that evoke the life and times of this rugged and romanticized figure. For example, the poem "Fausto" by Estanisláo del Campo (1834–1880) is a *gaucho* version of the Faust legend in which a man sells his soul. Literary critics consider "Martin Fierro," a poem on *gaucho* life by José Hernández (1834–1886), to be the national epic. The poem decries the fencing of the Pampas and the resulting loss of the *gaucho* lifestyle. In an earlier essay titled "Facundo," Domingo Faustino Sarmiento (1811–1888) describes how rural life of the Pampas shaped the national character. This essay became popular and helped Sarmiento win the presidency in 1868. Many folk songs about the *gaucho* also come from 19th century.

Not all 19th-century writings were about the *gaucho*. For example, Esteban Echeverría (1805-1851) wrote a short story titled "The Slaughterhouse" that is still required reading in some Argentine schools. The story protests the ruthless dictatorship of Jean Manuel de Rosas. The rest of the world was not as interested in the *gaucho* and Argentina's political problems as were Argentines. Consequently, Argentine writers did not reach a world audience until recent decades.

The National Congress meets in the capital city of Buenos Aires. Members are elected by popular vote.

5

Government and Politics

The Argentine population, which is extremely opinionated, is probably one of the most politically active and impassioned of all Latin Americans.

Foster, et al., *Culture and Customs of Argentina*

GOVERNMENT TERRITORY

Argentina was put together like a jigsaw puzzle. The puzzle began to take shape in the 1700s when Spanish Bourbon kings tried to improve the administration of their colonies. They split off large areas of the Viceroyalty of Peru to create two new administrative units. To the north, Bourbon reformers separated the Viceroyalty of Nueva Granada in 1739. It included the area that would become the countries of Venezuela, Colombia, and Ecuador. Bogotá (in Colombia) was the capital. To the south, in 1776, they created the Viceroyalty of Río La Plata with Buenos Aires as its capital. This new Viceroyalty, in addition to Argentina, included what are today Paraguay, Uruguay, and the southern half of Chile.

Argentines officially declared their independence from Spain in 1816. They formed the United Provinces of Río de la Plata. This union also was supposed to include the territories of modern-day Paraguay and Uruguay. However, Paraguay already had declared independence from Spain. It fought off an Argentine army that marched north to claim the country as part of the United Provinces. Uruguay did not wish to be part of the United Provinces either. However, it was unable to break free and became a semi-independent possession of the United Provinces.

Paraguay was unsatisfied with being merely independent. For trading purposes, it also wanted to control Uruguay in order to gain a direct outlet to the Atlantic Ocean. Pursuing this goal, the Paraguayan army invaded Uruguay and eventually pushed into southern Brazil as well. In response, Argentina, Uruguay, and Brazil formed the Triple Alliance and fought Paraguay from 1865 to 1870. In the end, Paraguay was defeated. Uruguay emerged from the war as an unofficial country that both Argentina and Brazil desired. Rather than go to war, however, the two countries decided to recognize Uruguay's independence. They negotiated its official statehood in 1928. Uruguay thus became a buffer state, or barrier to political friction that might develop between the two larger and more powerful countries.

PROVINCES

Recognition of Uruguay as an independent state established the general boundaries of modern Argentina. The final pieces of Argentina's political jigsaw are its provinces. As the country's total population grew and its settlement spread over more territory, more local government was needed to run the country. By 1858, the government grew to include 20 provinces. All were squeezed into the northern part of the country, because most settlement was limited to that area. The government's policy of removing indigenous peoples and recruiting European immigrant farmers to replace them increased the spread of settlement. As a result, the size and number of provinces grew to 22 by 1884. The newest province, the island province of Tierra del Fuego, was created in 1990. For the first time, Argentina established provincial boundaries in all of Patagonia, the southernmost region.

Modern Argentina consists of a federal district (the city of Buenos Aires), 23 provinces. Officially, the government also claims the island territories in the south Atlantic, including the Falkland Island (or *Las Malvinas*) and South Georgia Islands. However, the United Kingdom disputes these claims and presently administers all the islands. Argentina also claims a wedge-shaped section of Antarctica, but territorial claims to this continent are on hold by international agreement.

FEDERAL REPUBLIC

Argentina is a republic, meaning its citizens elect politicians to represent their interests in government. The country's constitution, adopted in 1853, gives all citizens aged 18 or older the right to vote in elections. The constitution also provides for a federal system of government. A federal system is a union of self-governing provinces (or states as in the United States) that has a central government. The federal government runs the country as a whole, but provincial governments take care of local matters. The constitution divides the federal and provincial governments into three branches: executive, legislative and judicial. Separation of powers among these three branches allows for a system of checks and balances similar to that of the three branches of the U.S. government.

The federal government meets in Buenos Aires, the nation's capital. Buenos Aires is an autonomous Federal District, in which residents elect their own politicians to represent them in the federal government. Together, the district and province of Buenos Aires control national political life. They have more than one-third of the country's population. They are also the core of nation's business and financial power.

Operation of provincial governments mirrors that of the federal government. Each province has its own capital or seat of government. Citizens of each province elect a governor to lead the provincial government. They also elect members to serve in their province's legislative and judicial branches.

BRANCHES OF THE FEDERAL GOVERNMENT

A president heads the executive branch of the federal government and usually dominates national politics. The president chooses a cabinet of ministers. According to the 1994 changes to the Argentine constitution, the president is elected for a 4-year term in office and is entitled to run for a second successive term. The 1994 constitution also introduced the role of cabinet chief—a position comparable to that of a prime minister— in the executive branch. This change was designed to limit presidential power. However, the president is still very much in charge, as he or she chooses the cabinet chief. The cabinet chief supervises governmental matters nationwide and coordinates dealings between the executive and legislative branches. The cabinet chief also oversees the various cabinet ministers. Each minister is in charge of one major aspect of government. There are ministers of defense, health, economy, education, and production. Ministers also oversee social development; justice, security, human rights, foreign affairs, and international trade.

The legislative branch is the National Congress. The Congress is bicameral, meaning it has two bodies of legislators: a Senate and a Chamber of Deputies. Citizens elect members of both bodies. The Senate has 72 members (Senators): three members from each province and the Federal District. Senators serve six-year terms. One-third of the Senate is elected every

President Eduardo Duhalde worked hard to solve Argentina's economic problems. In 2002, he obtained a $20 billion loan from the International Monetary Fund.

two years. The Chamber of Deputies has 257 members. The number of deputies from each province is proportional to the size of its population. In other words, provinces with large populations have more Deputies than do provinces with small populations. The Deputies have four-year terms with half the seats renewable every three years. There are no term limits, meaning voters may reelect Senators and Deputies to an unlimited number of successive terms.

The judiciary branch is separate and independent from the executive and legislative branches under the constitution. The president appoints the nine federal Supreme Court judges. The Senate votes to accept or reject the appointments. The Supreme Court may declare legislative acts illegal.

POLITICAL PARTIES

The largest political group is the Justicialist Party, also called the Perónist party in recognition of Juan Perón who founded it in 1945. The second party is the *Union Civica Radical* (UCR), or Radical Civic Union. The UCR is Argentina's oldest party. It was founded in 1890. Traditionally, the UCR has received support from the urban middle-class, whereas support for the Perónist party has come from labor. Smaller parties, such as Action for the Republic (AR) and the more leftist-leaning Argentina for a Republic of Equals (ARI), occupy various positions on the political spectrum. Political parties often create alliances among themselves to win elections. The alliances usually disband after they lose elections.

Historically, organized labor has supported the Perónist party. As a leader of coups and a police force for dictators, the military has played a significant role in national politics. However, labor's political power has declined, and the armed forces are firmly under civilian rule because of 1994 amendments to the constitution. Spurned by the public after a period of bloody rule (1976–1983), the Argentine military today is a scaled back, volunteer force.

NATIONAL POLITICS

A very ugly era of Argentine politics ended in the early 1980s with the end of the Falkland Islands War and the Dirty War. Democracy returned in 1983 when Argentines elected Raúl Alfonsín, a member of the UCR party, as their new president. Alfonsín undertook several measures to win the confidence of the Argentine people. He demoted or removed military officers who participated in the two wars. He curbed the power of trade unions by decreasing workers' wages. He also brought former *junta* members to trial. Government prosecutors charged them with approving the murder, torture, and kidnapping of the *desaparecidos* and of mishandling the Falkland Islands War. The courts gave many of the former junta leaders stiff jail sentences, which were eventually commuted to time served.

Alfonsín completed his six-year term of office in 1989. To replace him, Argentines elected Carlos Raúl Menem of the Perónist party. Menem promised to reduce the national debt and inflation. He achieved his first promise by reducing inflation to less than 10 percent by the mid-1990s. However, the national debt remained large. Menem used his popularity and political skills to persuade the legislature to amend the Constitution of 1853. The amendment allowed Argentines to elect a president to two four-year terms, rather than one six-year term. Argentine voters reelected Menem to a second (four-year) term that began in 1995. His second term, however, was not as successful as his first. Corruption scandals plagued his administration. Moreover, his economic policies led to severe recession, increased national debt, and higher unemployment. Menem's poor second term ruined the Perónist party's chances of staying in power.

Former Buenos Aires mayor Fernando de la Rúa captured the presidency in 1999. He was the candidate of the Alliance Party. His government faced a huge budget deficit passed down by Menem and his predecessors. De la Rúa's presidency was unpopular, as he had to take necessary but unpopular measures to reduce the government's deficit. He raised taxes and reduced government spending by making massive cuts in social programs. To keep money in reserve, he froze withdrawals from personal savings accounts. People rioted in the streets, demanding a new election.

De le Rúa resigned abruptly in late 2000. Congress held an emergency session and chose Eduardo Duhalde, a Perónist, to be president starting in January 2002. President Duhalde faced the same challenges that his predecessors faced: inflation, national debt, unemployment, and government corruption. He suspended payments on Argentina's foreign debt and promised elections in 2003.

ARGENTINE-CHILEAN BOUNDARY DISPUTES

Territorial boundaries are often imperfect and are sometimes the subject of dispute among nations. The Argentine-Chilean boundary is a classic case in point. Two instances concerning this boundary dispute serve as examples of how countries can work together to peacefully resolve their differences.

The first case involves a dispute using the crest of the Andes as the boundary line. Both Argentina and Chile prepared for war in the late 19th century. However, ultimately they agreed to ask the Queen of England to settle the dispute. A resolution was reached in 1902. In gratitude for the averting war, the peoples of the two countries built a 26-foot tall bronze "Christ of the Andes" statue in Uspallata Pass, the main route through the mountains between Buenos Aires and central Chile.

Argentines and Chileans also used diplomacy to solve a second boundary dispute. The issue was over which country owned a cluster of three barren islands south of Tierra del Fuego. The dispute began in the 1840s and almost led to war between the two nations in 1978. Although the islands did not have any value themselves, the country that owned them would be entitled to fishing and mineral rights to a large area in the South Atlantic. To their credit, the two countries asked Pope John Paul II to settle the dispute. His representatives concluded that the three islands belonged to Chile, and the two countries signed a treaty agreeing to the Pope's decision in 1985.

RECENT INTERNATIONAL RELATIONS

Argentina's prestige among nations hit rock bottom due to the violent policies of its military government that ruled from

1976 to 1983. Since then, the country has been working to improve its image by supporting U.N. military peacekeeping efforts. For example, Argentina was the only Latin American country to take part in the United Nations Gulf War and all phases of restoring democracy to Haiti. Moreover, the United States designated Argentina as a major non-NATO (North Atlantic Treaty Organization) ally in January 1998. Argentina also supports efforts to improve human rights in Cuba. It is also cooperating in the fight against drug trafficking.

Argentina is also helping fight the War on Terrorism. For example, it worked with American intelligence officials to locate suspected Al Qaeda terrorist cells in Misiones Province in early 2003. This province is in the geographic center of the Triple Frontier where Argentina, Brazil, and Paraguay meet. According to Larry Rohter of the *New York Times*, the Triple Frontier "has long been the busiest contraband and smuggling center in South America, a corrupt, chaotic place where just about anything from drugs and arms to pirated software and bootleg whisky are available to anyone who can pay the price." This sort of environment attracts terrorists seeking to purchase various illegal arms, ammunition, and explosives.

Argentina has also been improving its image and influence with its South American neighbors since the early 1980s. The country settled its lingering border dispute with Chile in 1985. Through diplomatic efforts, it also helped to discourage military takeovers in Ecuador and Paraguay. Argentine diplomats have also helped broker a peace treaty between Peru and Ecuador. Moreover, the country has restored diplomatic relations with the United Kingdom, which were broken after the Falkland Islands War.

Additionally, Argentina has revitalized its relationship with its neighbors by participating in the Southern Cone Common Market, or Mercosur. In an effort to enhance political and economic stability in the region, Mercosur approved a plan that allows people to live and work in any other member country

The Mothers of the Plaza de Mayo march through the streets of Buenos Aires carrying pictures of their missing children. The mothers demand to know what happened to the people who disappeared during the country's military rule, which lasted from 1976 to 1983.

and possess the same rights as the citizens of those nations. The agreement is scheduled to go into effect after all members' legislatures sign on to the plan. Once the plan is in place, immigrants will be able to apply immediately for amnesty that will permit them to remain where they are without fear of deportation. They will be able to work, study, open bank accounts, use social services, invest and buy real estate in any of the countries just as if they were citizens.

PROTESTS AGAINST THE GOVERNMENT

Protests against the government, regardless of the party in power, are a way of life in Argentina. Argentines protest for various reasons. The Madres de la Plaza de Mayo (Plaza de Mayo Mothers) meets each Thursday at the Plaza. They have met since the 1970s, demanding to know why their children were "disappeared" by the military government of 1976–1983.

The Thursday protests echo those of various Jewish groups who demonstrate each Monday morning in the Plaza. They demand that those guilty of the 1994 car bombing of the Jewish Cultural Center be brought to justice.

Other Argentines hold less regular but more volatile protests against the government's inability to heal an ailing economy. These protesters and others also criticize the corruption that spurs many of the country's economic troubles. They argue that poverty and low incomes are major factors behind corruption. (Public officials, including police, judges and bureaucrats earn relatively low salaries, making them susceptible to bribes.)

Argentina's national leaders are sometimes guilty of corruption. President Duhalde, for example, was linked to corruption charges when he was governor of Buenos Aires Province. Two of Duhalde's predecessors, de la Rúa and Menem, also were involved in corruption scandals. Menem still faces legal problems resulting from his sale of arms to countries where the United Nations prohibits such sales. Swiss banks have partially frozen his accounts, which reportedly hold more than $10 million, because of the charges.

Unfortunately, most of Argentina's population seems to accept corruption. They view it as simply part of the culture. This attitude may take years to change. Many observers describe Argentines as people who are avid about politics, but deeply cynical about government.

Argentina has some of the most fertile farmland in the world. This worker is harvesting grapes for a local winery.

6

Argentina's Economy

A rgentina is comprised of four economic regions: Pampas, Northeastern, Northwestern, and Patagonia. Exports of agricultural products are the mainstay of the country's economy. The country's main economic relations are with the United States, Europe, and its neighbors, Brazil, Chile, Uruguay, and Paraguay. Argentines enjoy a high standard of living compared to other South Americans. Fully half the population considers itself middle class. Serious economic problems exist, however. The country's business community had foreign trade problems in the 1990s, although this trade now seems to be improving. Most serious is the government's huge external debt, a problem that has no easy solution. Increasingly, more people throughout the country are living in poverty. The interior regions outside of the Pampas have the lowest incomes and fewest jobs.

PAMPAS

The Pampas is South America's wealthiest agricultural area. The region's fertile soil is the primary source of this wealth. Outside influences also are important. During the late 1800s, European prosperity created surplus capital, particularly in Britain. The British transplanted some of their newfound capital and business methods to the Pampas. Additionally, they exported technology especially suitable to the grassy, windswept plains of the Pampas—the windmill and barbed wire. These innovations spurred the grazing and breeding of high-quality beef cattle. Additionally, refrigerated meatpacking plants (*frigorífico*) replaced beef-salting plants (*saladero*). By the close of the 19th century, railroads joined the main cities of the Pampas to Buenos Aires. From the port of Buenos Aires, swift ships with onboard refrigeration delivered fresh beef and other foodstuffs to markets across the Atlantic.

Today, the main products of the Pampas—hides (for leather), beef, wool, and wheat—have an important place on the world's marketplace. The "Wet Pampa," the more humid eastern part of the region, is more productive than the "Dry Pampa" to the west. The Wet Pampa produces most of the nation's agricultural exports. It is the granary of South America, with soybeans, alfalfa, corn, sunflowers, and flax as the principal crops. The main crop in the Dry Pampa is wheat. Cattle and sheep ranches exist throughout the region.

In addition to agriculture, the region is home to most of Argentina's principal industrial cities. Buenos Aires is located on the eastern edge of the Pampas. This huge port city is the country's chief financial, industrial, commercial, and social center. It is also the country's distribution hub and trade outlet. Railroads link the city to other urban areas in the Pampas and the interior regions. Additionally, a great inland river system links the city with Uruguay, Paraguay, and Brazil. Buenos Aires is the nation's most heavily industrialized city due to its favorable Atlantic coast location. Agricultural products from throughout the country are brought to Buenos Aires, processed, and then exported to other countries. The city has giant flourmills and meatpacking and refrigeration plants. There are also automobile factories and oil refineries. Additionally, Buenos Aires is a center for printing, publishing, metalworking, and machine building. Other industries include the manufacture of chemical, beverage, textile, clothing, and tobacco products. Major exports from Buenos Aires include meat, leather goods, dairy products, wool, wheat, corn, soybeans and soybean oil, petroleum, and automobiles. Ships carry these products to trading partners in South and North America, Europe, and elsewhere.

There are several other important cities elsewhere on the Pampas, each of which grew in economic importance because of its location. La Plata, east of Buenos Aires, draws business from its giant neighbor and is an important meatpacking and oil-refining center. Mar del Plata enjoys a seaside location near the mouth of the Rio de la Plata estuary. It is a fishing port and fashionable resort for foreign tourists and summer vacationers from Buenos Aires. Rosario, Argentina's third-largest city, is located on the Paraná River. Consequently, the city is a huge grain port. It is also an important iron- and steel-producing and oil-refining center. Santa Fe is located up river from Rosario. This city also depends on the Paraná River traffic, but the boats must be smaller, as the river grows smaller and shallower upstream. Situated inland and on the northern edge of the Pampas, Santa Fe processes grain, vegetable oils, and meats.

Córdoba, the nation's second-largest city, is located on the western edge of the Pampas. This city is important because it is a highway and railroad transportation hub between the Pampas and the outer regions. The transportation system brings raw materials and products from the surrounding region to Córdoba for assembly and processing. It is a center for automobile, leather, textile, and glass manufacturing, and food processing. Bahía Blanca is on the southern edge of the Pampas. Like Buenos Aires, it is a port city on the Atlantic coast that specializes in oil refining. Ranchers raise sheep and livestock in the southern Pampas, so Bahía Blanca is also a center for meatpacking and wool processing. Cargo ships transport products from Bahía Blanca to distant lands.

INTERIOR ECONOMIC REGIONS

The interior regions have better connections to the Pampas than they do among themselves. Their populations and economies are smaller because of limited natural resources and remote locations. There is only a scattering of oases and favorable river valleys. Mining and tourism provide badly needed jobs and income. Historically, people in these poorer regions have migrated to cities in the Pampas seeking jobs.

The Northeastern economic region corresponds to the Northeastern physical division. Consequently, it has three parts. From east to west, they are: the Paraná Plateau, Mesopotamia, and the Gran Chaco. A transportation system links the three subregions. All roads carry merchandise to and from Santa Fe, the northern gateway to the Pampas. Small boats also carry products on the Paraná and Uruguay rivers. These boats carry products back and forth between the Northeastern region and the Pampas. The largest towns— Formosa, Resistencia, Corrientes, Paraná and Posadas—are located along the Paraná River, reflecting the economic importance of the river. People now use roads more than the rivers to travel between the region's cities and towns. The Northeast exports a variety of agricultural products. The highest, wettest part, the Paraná Plateau, has a dense forest cover. Timber, paper (from processed wood), and *yerba maté* are the chief exports. The lower, warmer Mesopotamia area exports tobacco, citrus, and a few cattle. The relatively dry Gran Chaco exports wood products, cattle, cotton, and sunflower oil.

The dry Northern Andean region lies west of the Pampas and Gran Chaco. Scattered throughout the region's great dry stretches are small but highly productive agricultural valleys, such as Jujuy, Salta, Tucumán, San Juan, and Mendoza. The importance of these valley oases greatly increased after railroads linked them to Buenos Aires. These links opened markets outside the region for several products, including wine, sugar, fruits, and corn. Livestock ranching, especially of cattle and sheep, also is important. The mining of oil, lead, zinc, tin, copper, and salt provides badly needed employment in the region. Mendoza and Tucumán are major industrial areas engaged in food processing, oil refining, and chemical production. Mendoza is also a tourist gateway to Andean summer and winter recreation areas.

Patagonia—a vast, bleak, and windswept plateau—occupies the southern part of Argentina. This region is sparsely populated and underdeveloped. Sheep ranching (chiefly for wool) is the principal economic activity. Additionally, coal, oil and natural gas production are important. In the foothills of the Patagonian Andes, a series of dams on the Limay and Neuquén rivers generate low-cost electrical power. Power lines carry this hydroelectric energy to Buenos Aires. The poor soils of Patagonia and its cool, dry climate limit crop production. Descendants of hardy Welsh settlers practice irrigated agriculture in the Negro and Colorado River valleys. There are several river port communities on the Atlantic coast.

ARGENTINA'S AVERAGE INCOME

There are several ways to determine the strength of a country's economy. One is its gross domestic product (GDP), the value of all goods and services produced in a country in a given year. Per capita GDP can be determined by dividing a country's GDP by its population. According to the *World Fact Book*, a U.S. government publication, Argentina, in 2001, had the second-largest GDP ($453 billion) in South America (Brazil has the largest). Argentina also had an average income of $12,000 in that year, the highest in South America. Nevertheless, Argentina also has the highest unemployment rate in South America. Unemployment was 25 percent in 2001; underemployment (people with part-time or very low paying jobs) is much higher. In fact, nearly 40 percent of the country's population was living below the poverty level. In South America, only Columbia, Ecuador, and Peru have higher levels of poverty.

These numbers suggest that a huge number of people have no jobs or have jobs that do not earn enough money to pay for sufficient food, clothing, shelter, and healthcare. Additionally, the fact that Argentina leads South America in average incomes is misleading. The average income in the United States is three times higher ($36,000), so that most U.S. families can live in comfort. In contrast, prices for such items as cars, televisions, and other "luxury" items in Argentina are very high. After paying for basic essentials, most Argentines have little or no extra income to purchase them. In other words, many Argentines, even many who have jobs, are barely getting by.

> You see me digging through the garbage—what else can I say? I have to choose between feeding my children and clothing them. If they don't have clothes, they can't go to school . . . Today it's impossible to get milk for a baby! It takes me an hour, but sometimes I walk to the office of social services to see if they can help me. They never have anything. Now there are

More than 35 percent of Argentines live in poverty. Poor children search dumps for trash they can sell.

going to be elections. But why should we waste our time and energy to go and cast a vote? To elect another delinquent to office? There are times when I want to pick up and go, just pack everything up and leave here. I don't know where to.

Felicia Webb, "Barely Getting By in Argentina,"
New York Times Magazine

The previous quote is from a mother picking through trash in a garbage dump outside Buenos Aires. Her words speak volumes about the catastrophe of Argentina's economy. Yet, the country's financial system is actually better now than it was in the late 1980s when inflation (rising prices) reached 200 percent per month.

Argentina once had a booming economy. At the beginning of the 20th century, it was the world's leading exporter of foodstuffs. Its economy was second only to that of the United States in the Western Hemisphere. By the time Juan Perón rose to power in 1947, however, Argentina's economy was spiraling steadily downward. Perón caused some of the troubles by giving the state-run workers' union that he created hefty wage increases. (He increased their wages to win the workers' votes at election time.) Agreeing to strong union demands became a matter of policy in the following decades. Paying higher wages to workers raised the costs of producing goods. The factory owners then raised prices of their goods so they could continue making profits. However, the higher price of goods renewed workers' demands for even higher wages.

To meet demands for increased wages, the government began to print extra money. This practice caused prices to soar in the 1980s, devastating the economy. In the meantime, the government was borrowing money from other countries to pay for expensive public works projects, such as building highways, bridges, and hospitals. The country's economy was perilously close to collapse. Foreign investors began to pull their money out of the country. President Menem's government took steps to reduce inflation to manageable levels in the late 1980s. Nevertheless, the country's economy continued to suffer from lack of investment capital. Many factories and businesses closed, and thousands of people lost their jobs. The government ordered banks to close temporarily because they did not have enough cash to cover withdrawals. Once known for its high standard of living and affordable food prices, Argentina saw many of its middle-class citizens plunging into poverty. This problem persists today. According to news reports in 2002, among the growing ranks of rubbish sorters were electricians, carpenters, construction workers, and former office workers.

EXPORT TRADE AND BUDGET DEFICITS

Argentina's economy depends heavily on export trade. More than half of the country's exports go to Brazil, Chile, United States, Spain, and the Netherlands. For years, Argentina earned more money from its exports than it spent on imports. But economic reforms and restructuring left the country with a trade deficit in the 1990s. A trade deficit occurs when the value of a country's exports is less than that of its imports. When trade deficits occur annually, business owners have little money to pay employees, or to invest in their operations. Fortunately, Argentina had trade surpluses in 2000 and 2001. For example, the value of imported goods equaled $23.8 billion in 2001, whereas exported goods were valued at $26.5 billion. The balance was a surplus of $2.7 billion for that year.

Although Argentina's balance of trade appears to be improving, the government has had a long history of budget deficits. Annually, Argentina spends more money than it collects in taxes and fees. For example, the government's revenues in 2000 amounted to $44 billion, but it spent $48 billion. Thus, the government owed $4 billion for that year. To pay such deficits, the government borrows money from banks in other countries. Bank loans to pay Argentina's budget deficit have been adding up for decades. The country's total debt, or money it owes in unpaid loans, was about $155 billion in 2001, the second-highest in South America—only Brazil owed more money.

HARD ROAD TO ECONOMIC RECOVERY

As the 21st century begins, Argentina's government and banks do not have money to repay debts or to give back money that people have deposited in bank accounts. Argentina has few options left to rescue its financial system. It needs access to money to stimulate the economy. The government is trying to generate money by improving the country's trade surplus, by attracting foreign investment, and by obtaining low-interest loans from the International Monetary Fund (IMF).

In an attempt to improve its trade surpluses and thereby free up more money for its economy, Argentina joined with Brazil, Paraguay, and Uruguay to form Mercosur in 1991. (Bolivia and Chile are associate members.) Mercosur (Spanish acronym for Southern Cone Common Market) is the world's third-largest free-trade area, representing 250 million people. (Countries in a free-trade area charge no or very small taxes on goods they exchange in order to reduce the prices of the goods.) Nearly 40 percent of Argentina's exports and about 30 percent of its imports involved Mercosur members in 2001. So far, Argentina's economy shows a slight surplus in this trade.

Argentina welcomes Foreign Direct Investment (FDI) to improve its economy. FDI means that foreign companies own capital (businesses, land, buildings, and equipment) in Argentina. With nearly $18 billion invested by 2001, the United States is Argentina's main source of FDI. U.S. companies have concentrated their investments in telecommunications, petroleum and gas, electric energy, financial services, chemicals, food processing, and vehicle manufacturing. Private firms from Spain, France, and Chile have also invested large amounts of money directly into Argentina's economy.

Unfortunately, many financial experts say that the FDI and export trade are not providing enough money to rescue Argentina's economy. They believe the government also needs money from long-term, low-interest loans from the International Monetary Fund (IMF). Countries are eligible for such loans if they establish policies that are fiscally responsible and follow specific financial guidelines, such as raising taxes, cutting government spending, and balancing deficits to reduce their national debts. Many Argentine politicians, however, are unwilling to make the hard decisions that are necessary to improve the country's economy.

Soccer is the most popular sport in the country. Argentina won the World
Cup in 1978 and 1986.

Living in Argentina Today

Argentines are socially outgoing by nature. Visiting with family members, relatives, and friends is their most important leisure activity. Getting together on Sundays to eat pasta or have a barbeque is a tradition. Argentines also like to spend time after work hours improving their homes, watching television, or taking strolls in the neighborhood plaza. Going to movies is also popular. A smaller number of people go to the theater because these tickets are more expensive than the cinema. Occasionally, adults combine music, dancing, and nightlife. A typical night out starts with dinner at a nightclub beginning about 9 P.M. Nightclubs do not open until then, but they stay open all night. After sunrise, when the nightclubs close, partygoers usually stop at small cafés or go home for breakfast before falling into bed.

Aside from politics, soccer (*fútbol* in Spanish) is probably

Argentines' greatest obsession. British sailors introduced the game in the 1860s. Later, the large British community in Buenos Aires organized the first soccer league in the country. About 20 professional men's soccer teams now capture the attention of Argentina, 13 of them in Greater Buenos Aires. The soccer season runs from March to December. The best players play on the national team, which is often a contender for the World Cup. This competition takes place every four years. Teams from all over the world compete in a series of games for the honor of winning a huge silver trophy—the World Cup—for their country.

Argentina won the cup in 1978 and 1986 and was runner-up in 1990 after losing in the final game to West Germany. Experts rank Argentina's team among the best in the world every year. They ranked it second behind France in 2002. Surprisingly, neither team reached the final game of the World Cup that year.

The best male players in youth leagues also play on a national team. Players must be under 20 years of age. Every two years, the team competes in the World Youth Soccer Championship series. In 2001, Argentina's team placed second after losing the championship game to the French. Many Argentines also play tennis, rugby, and cricket, (all games imported from Britain), and American basketball. Popular spectator sports include horseracing, polo (also of British origin), boxing, and Formula 1 automobile racing.

FAMILY LIFE

Grandparents often live with the family of one of their sons or daughters. When a family has a party or a picnic, they often invite all the cousins and uncles and aunts who bring their relatives or close friends. More than one-third of the nation's entire population lives in one city (Buenos Aires) and its suburbs, making it is far easier for relatives to get together than it is in the United States.

Young people usually go to college in their hometowns, so they remain at home longer than students do in the United States. Even after graduation, young people usually live at home until they get married. In recent years, the number of sons and daughters living at home has been increasing due to the poor economy and lack of jobs. The long stay at home means the generation gap is far less clear than in some countries. Young and old are used to one another's company. They share news and ideas comfortably. Parents and grandparents are accessible. Like young people everywhere, Argentine youth must still learn to find their own way in the world.

Families tend to move less than they do in the United States, so neighborhoods are more stable. Children have the same classmates throughout their schooling. Parents and children of different families celebrate birthdays and holidays, have picnics, and take field trips together. The common bond of shared experience cements friendships in communities for life.

In recent years, a weak economy has been testing the strength of Argentine families and their communities. Economic problems have forced fathers and sons to move from home to take jobs in other communities. Many other male family members are unemployed. As a result, more mothers and daughters are seeking jobs than ever before. Women now comprise about 40 percent of the labor force, as more men are unemployed or absent from the home. Consequently, women are now the main income earners in one-third of the households. Additionally, more than half of all university students are female, as more women are seeking higher paying professional jobs.

FAMILY VACATIONS

Argentine families like to take vacations. They have been doing so since the 1930s, first by train then by car and airplane as the transportation system improved. With the beginning of commercial airliner transportation in the 1960s, they have shared their vacation spots with tourists from many other countries.

Jet airline travel made Argentina accessible to both winter and summer vacationers from Europe and North America. During the past decade, however, many Argentine families have been unable to afford vacations due to a worsening economy.

Mar del Plata, on the Atlantic coast about four hours by car or bus from Buenos Aires, is Argentines' favorite summertime destination. Argentines refer to Mar del Plata as *La Perla del Atlántico* (the Pearl of the Atlantic) for its impressive seascapes. Rock music, tango dancing, sunny beaches, sightseeing, snorkeling, windsurfing, and fishing draw them to the city. Overcrowding in recent years has pushed vacationers away from Mar del Plata to nearby coastal towns and beaches that are more solitary. In recent years, many Argentine travelers have been vacationing in nearby Uruguay to avoid crowded beaches.

Argentines who enjoy hills or mountains seek out Córdoba and its nearby mountain landscapes. This large city has the country's finest examples of colonial buildings. The Central Sierras rise out of the Pampas to the west of the city. Mountain lakes, surging streams, and inspirational scenery attract hikers, horseback riders, and fishing enthusiasts. During the summer, mountain villages hold folk festivals that are suggestive of festivals in Germany. The Oktoberfest beer festival organized by the German community in Villa General Belgrano is the most famous.

The third most popular vacation area is the Lake District. This district includes two national parks: Nahuel Huapí, pronounced "nowel wapi" and Lanín. These parks are nestled side-by-side in glacially scoured Andean slopes. The parks are about a thousand miles to the southwest of Buenos Aires and a few hours by air (or a long trip by car or train). Since the late 1950s, this area has been attracting alpine skiers. It has skiing and snow conditions very similar to those of New England and the Rockies in winter. Skiers from the Northern Hemisphere who like to ski the year-round come here in July and August, the Southern Hemisphere's winter season. The district is a fisherman's paradise as well. Sparkling streams and crystal lakes are

Argentina's mountain-fed rivers and streams attract fishing enthusiasts from all over the world.

swimming with trout and salmon. As in the Central Sierras, a European influence is evident in villages of the Lake District. For example, entrance to the Nahuel Huapí National Park is through Bariloche, a colorful Swiss-style village.

A fourth vacation spot is Iguazú Falls. The falls are on the Paraná River near the point where Argentina, Brazil, and Paraguay meet. A popular vacation guidebook describes these falls as "one of the most awe-inspiring sights on the planet." The falls consist of more than 1,200 cascades that plunge nearly 270 feet (82 meters) in a display that dwarfs North America's Niagara Falls in beauty and size. The falls send mist hundreds of feet into the sky and their roar can be heard from a mile away. A few miles upstream is the huge Itaipú Dam. This vast concrete structure is the world's largest hydroelectric power plant. More than one million people visit Itaipú Dam and Iguazú Falls each year.

THE PLAZA

When they are not at home with their families, at work, in school, or on vacation, Argentines like to spend time in their town's "Spanish" plaza. Spanish colonists tried to recreate Spain's towns and cities in the New World. Therefore, one of the most basic elements of Argentina's towns is the plaza. Plazas are open-air squares. Some plazas have a small park lined with flowers and trees. Nearly always, they have a water fountain or a prominent statue of an important historical figure. Spaniards also included in their towns an orderly, rectangular grid of streets that enter plazas from all sides. Thus, plazas have easy access and are the focus of important activities. They are convenient gathering places for townspeople to converse, do business, or just relax. Weddings, public speeches, festivals, and other private and public activities take place here. Stores, churches, and offices are on the streets facing them or on nearby streets. Smaller towns have a single plaza, which is always located in the town centers. Larger towns usually have more than one plaza, with one central or main square and several smaller or neighborhood plazas.

The most famous plaza in Argentina is Plaza de Mayo in Buenos Aires. The town's founders laid it out in 1580. Spanish law dictated that they include a fort, church, jail, and *cabildo* (town hall). Each structure occupied a different side of the plaza. Since the late 1800s, there have been important changes in the classic Spanish street grid pattern that gave access to plazas. A spider web of railroads from Buenos Aires' growing suburbs to the city center interrupts the old grid pattern. City planners have also added subways, diagonal streets, and broad avenues to the classic pattern. (The system of subways, begun in 1913, was the first in Latin American.) Locations along these new transportation routes now have commercial activities that used to be prominent in plaza area.

Despite modern-day changes, the Plaza de Mayo remains

very important. It is the center of both federal and city govern-ment—the Casa Rosada (presidential palace) and the *Cabildo* (old town hall) are located there. Various other government buildings and Argentina's Stock Exchange are also there or nearby. The plaza is still a place for people to gather, visit, and carry out vital social and public activities.

THE *ESTANCIA*

The *estancia* (ranch) is the center of rural life. Vast stretches of unpopulated land separate these ranches from small towns. Narrow two-lane highways connect the towns. A visitor traveling the highways sees wheat and alfalfa fields, clusters of grazing animals, and an occasional side road, fence, and windmill. The side road is often unpaved and invariably connects distant *estancias* to the highway.

Traditional *estancias*, particularly those in the Pampas, are beautiful estates with entrance gates, wide arching driveways, swimming pools, tennis courts, riding stables, large flower gardens, and landing fields for private airplanes. These large landholdings employ 30 or more workers. The main house is for the owner and his family. Owners often maintain an additional residence, usually in Buenos Aires, and only spend weekends or summers on the ranch. Wealthy ranchers often send their children to expensive boarding schools in London or Paris. A resident manager is usually in charge of work on such an estate. He and his family live a large spacious house, which is often richly furnished. The workers' families live in modest quarters. Unmarried men live in a bunkhouse.

Life on the *estancia* has grown out of the tradition of raising livestock. The original owners were mostly Argentine *criollos*, whose main occupation was herding cattle, sheep, and horses. The size of an estate was tens of thousands of acres (hectares) of fenceless grassland. The rural economy has changed consider-ably since the early days. There has been a gradual decrease in the number of large estates as the family *estancia* has become fenced off and subdivided. (Argentine inheritance laws divide property among all children of a family.)

There is also a more diverse source of income now. Depending on its location and size, an *estancia* might grow wheat, alfalfa, corn, vegetables, or fruit, in addition to raising livestock. Fresh milk, vegetables, and fruit are in high demand in cities. Thus, dairy farming is more important than raising beef cattle or sheep near urban centers. On the outskirts of Buenos Aires, fresh vegetable farms have replaced *estancias.* The farms are as small as 25 to 30 acres (10 to 12 hectares) and have totally replaced livestock ranching. Additional farms as well as larger *estancias* have developed specialized production of fresh fruit (apples, pears, plums, and peaches) at the juncture of the Paraná and Uruguay rivers near Buenos Aires.

In interior provinces, where the environment is harsher and markets are more remote, large *estancias* have remained. They are still devoted almost exclusively to raising livestock. Life on these ranches is difficult. The climate is dry, soil is poor, and pasture is less nutritious. Ranchers rent some of the land to families who operate small ranches (*puestos*). They work for the *estancia* owner, but also raise a few vegetables and sheep, goats, cattle, or horses to eke out a living.

Many of the larger, more elegant *estancias* have fallen on hard economic times during the last few decades. Increasingly, to make ends meet, they rent rooms to foreign tourists and Argentine vacationers. Guests stay for a few days or several weeks, and watch or participate in the activities of the ranch. These modern-day *estancias* are similar to U.S. dude ranches.

FOOD

Argentines eat a small breakfast (*desayuno*). It usually consists of bread, toast or rolls and jam, with coffee, *yerba maté*, or cocoa. They eat lunch (*almuerzo*) at noon or 1 P.M. Dinner (*comida*) can be as late as 9 P.M., so late afternoon snacks are typical. A favorite snack is tasty *empanadas.* They are small pastries filled with cooked meat, tomato, onion, green olives, raisins, and hardboiled eggs. City dwellers commonly take an afternoon break in a small sidewalk café to enjoy a British-style cup of tea or *yerba maté* sipped through a straw from a gourd.

Lunch and dinner often consist of pizza, pasta, or meat dishes. Argentines eat more beef per capita than almost any other people. Not surprisingly, Argentine restaurants that specialize in beef dishes are most popular.

Due to widespread European influence, few dishes are typically Argentine. *Puchero* is an exception. The main ingredient of this dish is beef—boiled for several hours with fresh vegetables. Another country dish is *carbonada*, which is beef stew made with vegetables and fresh fruit, traditionally peaches and pears. A classic dessert (*postre*) is a soft caramel spread called *dulce de leche*. Argentines use *dulce de leche* much as Americans use peanut butter; they spread it on bread, crackers, and fruit. They also buy it in rolled pastry or as *cubanos* (thin cigar-shaped cones resembling Cuban cigars). Another dessert is *alfajores*, which are sandwiches, made of pastry stuck together with *dulce de leche*.

Argentines call a barbeque or cookout an *asado*. The name is from the word *asador*, the skewer on which early settlers and *gauchos* roasted meat. Meat is cooked in one large piece. The chef places beef or lamb ribs on a five-foot long skewer, then sticks the skewer into the ground at an angle so that the meat stands over the fire.

EDUCATION

Argentina's literacy rate—people over age 15 who can read and write—is 97 percent. (Only Uruguay has a higher literacy rate in Latin America.) There are three levels of education: primary, secondary, and higher. Schools are open from March to November. (This period includes fall, winter, and spring in the Southern Hemisphere). There is a three-month summer

Argentines enjoy cookouts, which they call an *asado*. Argentines consume more meat per person than almost any other country in the world.

break, from December to February. For issuing grades, teachers and professors use a number scale, rather than the letter scale used in the United States. A single course grade may range from 1 (insufficient) to 10 (superior). The lowest passing score is five. The average grade for all courses that a student takes in the school year determines whether he or she graduates to the next grade level.

Primary education is free and required for youngsters ages 6 to 15. Secondary education, for ages 15 to 18, is also free, but not required. According to a recent government study, only 14 percent of working adults completed their secondary education. National and private universities, as well as special teacher-training institutes, provide college education. Universities are traditionally free and open to anyone. Easy access to universities and a weak economy have created an oversupply of professionals, such as doctors and lawyers. Consequently, many graduates must work outside of their area of training. Public universities in Buenos Aires, Córdoba, and La Plata have reputations for excellence.

Children from poorer families have the highest dropout rates. The government offers small educational scholarships to the most needy youngsters to help them stay in school. Nevertheless, 40 percent of school dropouts come from families that are in the poorest one-fifth of the total population. Why so many children drop out is unclear. Educators say that one of the principal reasons is that youngsters do not find schooling relevant to their needs. They are no more likely to find a job at the end of their studies than if they were to drop out.

SOCIAL SECURITY, HEALTH, AND SOCIAL WELFARE

Argentina's social security system is similar to that of the United States. The only difference is that Argentina's system is bankrupt. Under the system, Argentine employers and workers pay taxes to fund social security. Current funds are used to make payments to people who have retired. Payment to a retiree is called a retirement pension. According to the system, future contributors will pay for future retirement pensions. However, retirees are living longer, so the number of contributors is falling while the number of retirees is growing. This creates a deficit in the pension fund. The Argentine government now pays the difference, but it is an added cost to running the country.

Free hospital clinics and various labor unions provide health services to workers. Argentina has the third-highest life expectancy among South American nations—74 years (Chile and Uruguay are higher). Nevertheless, medical services are uneven. There are too few doctors and hospitals in the country's poorer provinces. Additionally, infant mortality rates (the average number of deaths among children less than five years of age per 1,000 live births) in northwestern and northeastern Argentina is twice and sometimes three times higher than the rest of the country. High rates of infant deaths are due to poverty and malnutrition as well as poor health services in these regions.

Argentina's social welfare programs help poor people pay for food, medical care, housing, and education. However, the problem can seem overwhelming. According to studies, about 37 percent of the population in 2001 was living below the poverty line. Sadly, only 25 percent of this group received any form of direct public assistance. Moreover, some of the poorest areas receive the least help. The greatest rates of poverty are in the interior provinces, but rates of public assistance are greatest in Buenos Aires province. Indigenous people of rural areas in northern Argentina are often the most needy, as they live in remote areas away from public services.

TRANSPORTATION

Buenos Aires is the main transport center of Argentina. Most international airline flights, cargo ships, road and railroad traffic, telephone calls, and computer information begin or end here.

Argentine presidents since the 1880s believed that a transport network focusing on the capital would strengthen the nation's economy. They also assumed correctly that such a network would assure their political support from the country's most populous city and region. Their efforts made Buenos Aires the center for processing and shipping of nearly all goods produced in the country. As a result, almost everything passes through the capital.

Most city dwellers do not own a car and depend heavily on public transportation. They use subways (in Greater Buenos Aires), suburban railroads, and buses. These systems are seldom on time, and are overcrowded and deteriorating. There are broken windows, torn and damaged seats, and broken doors. Station facilities are poor, with graffiti and trash everywhere.

Moreover, in Greater Buenos Aires the systems do not inter-connect well. Railroad stops do not correspond with subway stations, for example. Buenos Aires suffers from severe traffic congestion due to the greater use of the automobile for commuting from surrounding suburbs. The noise, pollution, accidents, and congestion caused by the passenger cars severely damage the city's environment.

The airline network also focuses on Buenos Aires. Major airlines connect Buenos Aires to North America and Europe. Miami is the dominant gateway city between North America and Buenos Aires. There are four non-stop flights each day from Buenos Aires to Miami. Madrid and New York City are the second and third major non-stop international connec-tions. There are no international direct flights between foreign cities and interior cities. All freight and passengers traveling to the interior offload in Buenos Aires and reload onto smaller planes to complete the journey.

MEDIA AND ELECTRONIC COMMUNICATIONS

Argentina boasts about 30 major daily newspapers. Buenos Aires newspapers have the largest number of readers. Several have nationwide distribution, including *Clarín, La Nación, Crónica, Página 12, Ambito Financiero, La Razón, La Prensa* and *El Cronista. Clarín* has the largest readership. Main daily local non-Spanish written newspapers include the *Buenos Aires Herald* (English), *Argentinisches Tageblatt* (German) and *Le Monde Diplomatique* (French). Córdoba and Mendoza each have a major newspaper as well. Several Argentine newspapers use the Internet. The *Buenos Aires Herald* has an English-language Internet site.

The government used to own the telephone and television industries. Around 1990, however, it sold these industries to private firms to raise money for its failing economy. Foreign companies responded by investing in modern fiber-optic and digital networks. Most of the financing came from U.S.

telephone and cable companies. The number of telephone lines and wireless (cellular) telephones skyrocketed from 3 million in 1990 to 13 million in 2000. Additionally, a network of satellite receivers and digital cables now hooks up more than half the homes to news, educational, and entertainment programs from around the world. Argentina was one of the first Latin American countries to offer cable services such as HBO, CNN, and Cinemax from the United States. It also offers Mexico's "Eco" News Service, RAI from Italy, Televen from Venezuela, and TVE from Spain. There are also channels from Chile and France. Personal computers also increased from 235,000 in 1990 to 1,900,000 in 2000. The number of Internet users grew even faster during this period.

Despite these improvements, more than 65 percent of all installed computer and telecommunications equipment in Argentina is in the Greater Buenos Aires urbanized area. Most of this equipment is in the industrial, commercial, and service sectors. Many residents of Argentina cannot make international telephone calls or Internet connections from their homes.

WEIGHTS AND MEASURES, TIME, AND HOLIDAYS

Argentina uses the metric, rather than English, system of weights and measures. Grams and kilograms appear on packages, not ounces and pounds. Meters and kilometers designate distances, not feet and miles.

Argentina is three hours behind Greenwich Mean Time (or universal time). If it is 3 P.M. in Buenos Aires, it will be 6 P.M. in Greenwich, England and 1:00 P.M. in New York City. The country does not observe daylight savings time. In other words, Argentines do not turn their clocks ahead an hour in the spring and back an hour in the fall in order to have an extra hour of daylight during the summer.

The people of Argentina celebrate several public holidays at which time most shops, offices, and museums close. Argentines celebrate New Year's Day along with much of the rest of the world on January 1. Good Friday and Easter are also celebrated. On Easter Sunday, a meal is followed by an Easter egg hunt for the children. Mar del Plata and Córdoba are popular destinations for Argentines who take a vacation on these holidays. Other public holidays are: Labor Day (May 1); May Revolution or First Argentine Government Day (May 25), which commemorates the 1810 revolution against Spain; National Sovereignty Day (June 10); Flag Day (June 20); Independence Day (July 9); Anniversary of the Death of General San Martín (August 17); Columbus Day (October 12); Immaculate Conception Day (December 8); and Christmas (December 25).

There are numerous other special events and festivals. A few examples are: Carnaval, which occurs three days before Lent (Mardí Gras in New Orleans is the U.S. equivalent of Carnaval.); Virgin Mary of Luján Day (May 8), a day large numbers of believers pilgrimage to the basilica in Luján to honor the Virgin Mary; the Day of Traditional Culture (November 10), when Argentines celebrate the *gaucho* with parades and folkloric events.

As Argentina enters the twenty-first century, the country faces the daunting challenge of providing for its citizens. Young protesters took to the street in 2001 to demand better living conditions.

8

Argentina Looks Ahead

Don't cry for me Argentina
The truth is I never left you
All through my wild days
My mad existence
I kept my promise
Don't keep your distance

> *Don't Cry for Me Argentina.* Lyrics by Tim Rice.

Eva Perón, lead character in the Broadway musical and motion picture *Evita*, sings "Don't Cry for Me Argentina." Perón wanted no pity from her countrymen. But from a humane and spiritual perspective, maybe the people of Argentina are in need of those who will care enough to cry for them.

Argentina was one of the most successful nations in the world at the beginning of the 20th century. The country's location and diverse climate, vegetation, soils, and wildlife provided wide-ranging opportunities for economic growth. The population was healthy and well educated. Argentines had strong cultural and economic ties to Europe. The nation's future looked bright. Now, a century later, the country suffers from chronic debt, soaring school dropout rates, debilitating corruption, a shrinking middle class, a widening gap between rich and poor, and a generally disheartened population. An understanding of Argentina's economy, history, and geography shed light on how the country's present situation developed. Each perspective also points to possible future improvements.

The social scientist sees societies as having both positive and negative forces. Argentina's citizens enjoy a rich tradition in the fine arts (literature, music, and theater). They also take pleasure in various pastimes, foods, educational opportunities, and family and holiday activities. These shared experiences are positive social forces, as they tend to bring people together. Conversely, negative social forces in society keep people from enjoying life's experiences to the fullest. In Argentina, unemployment and the spread of poverty are weakening family ties. The government's bankrupt pension fund has all but ended plans for paid retirement. Corruption in government is out of control. In addition, interior cities have poor access to foreign markets, computers, and health and social welfare facilities.

The strength of Argentine society's negative forces is threatening the nation's future. However, the future is not beyond saving. Most of the problems that grip the country have economic origins. Argentina has the second-largest economy in South America (Brazil is first), and its government is taking difficult steps to ensure that it grows even more. Recent efforts have brought about improvements in fiscal management and a stronger trade balance. Social strains should subside in the future, as the economy improves.

The historian provides a second perspective on Argentina's

current situation. A historian views history as the crucible of ideas and traditions. These ideas and traditions help to create, stabilize, and develop nations. Unless a majority of a country's citizens support a certain set of ideas and traditions, a nation can break apart. Argentina, like most Latin American nations, did not become a country because its people agreed on any particular set of ideas and traditions. The country started because people desired freedom from colonial masters. Lacking common goals, Argentines struggled to establish order among diverse people and regions. Visionary leaders, who could have formulated a strong set of ideas and goals, failed to step forward during Argentina's critical beginning years. It took Argentines more than forty years to agree on a constitution! Unfortunately, Argentina did not have a "George Washington," "James Madison," or "Thomas Jefferson" to unite its people.

In the absence of visionary leaders, uneducated, ruthless *caudillos* rose to power and ran their own provinces as they saw fit. Regional politics led to disputes and violent clashes. National leaders during the early years, such as Rosas (1829–1852), ruled with the sword, not with fair and just laws. An unusual "Golden Age" of economic prosperity and internal peace occurred from 1880 to 1910. Major difficulties began anew when the Great Depression struck in 1930. Foreign loans to the government for investments in the country's infra-structure were not repaid and debts grew. After World War II, a long period of poor leadership and violence weakened the nation even further.

Argentines managed to stay together as a nation for different reasons. Defense against a common enemy in the Triple Alliance War brought them together. The lulling effects of economic prosperity, particularly during 1853–1930, also kept them together. However, many times in the past, Argentines could not agree. As a result, *caudillos* and dictators were the only people who could enforce order.

Argentines have grown to distrust government, but they

still must rely on it to solve serious economic and social problems. Free elections have been taking place since 1983. Argentina is gaining prestige as a peacekeeper and negotiator among its neighbors and nations globally. These are hopeful signs. For the first time since the early 1900s, Argentines' appear to have replaced violence with diplomacy at home and abroad in their quest for progress.

The geographer provides a third perspective on Argentina's situation. Geographers view the landscape as a painter's canvas on which history's ideas and traditions are recorded. In Argentina, decisions and circumstances along the way have created a landscape with serious regional imbalances and tensions. Argentina's diverse environment, ranging from subtropical to glacial, adds a fascinating and important physical backdrop. The grouping of Europeans, Jews, Arabs, and indigenous peoples superimposes a vibrant cultural mix. Contrasts between the bustle of the plaza and the wide-open spaces of the *estancia* add pleasing visual texture. But the geographical imbalances in Argentina focus our attention on the rise of Buenos Aires—its dominance and impact on the rest of the country.

Buenos Aires grew up on the shore of the Río de la Plata— the largest estuary along South America's eastern coast. The estuary is strategically situated on sea-lanes between the Atlantic and Pacific oceans. Spaniards used the location of Buenos Aires to their advantage. They chose this small backwater town as the capital of the Viceroyalty of Río de La Plata. Buenos Aires quickly became an engine of political power and economic growth. The Pampas' location next to Buenos Aires—as well as its settlement, mild climate, and rich soils—made this vast grassland one the world's major food-producing areas.

Today, the Pampas and Buenos Aires form the heartland of Argentina, the source of its greatest wealth, and the home of most of its population. The heartland's economic success notwithstanding, the interior provinces of Argentina remain relatively poor. Health, educational, and social welfare services are less developed. Jobs are fewer and incomes lower. Poverty is forcing people to move from rural to urban areas. Argentina's transportation system perpetuates the regional imbalance. It funnels **all** products from the interior for processing in Greater Buenos Aires. Cross-border trade could create new jobs in the interior cities, as trade would encourage jobs in manufacturing, packaging and transportation in those cities. Unfortunately, there are no railroads or quality highways to make this trade possible.

The imbalance in services and employment between Buenos Aires and interior provinces will be a difficult problem to fix in Argentina. This imbalance breeds anger among the interiors' inhabitants toward the richer coast and especially Buenos Aires. It also strengthens the long-held prejudices that *porteños* and people of the interior have for one another. However, Mercosur (the Southern Cone Common Market) plans to improve overland trade routes. Better trade links should bring more commerce and jobs to the interior provinces and reduce the imbalance.

Argentina will probably never regain the status it once had among nations. But there is great hope. After all, Argentina is a resourceful, beautiful, and interesting country populated by a proud, colorful, intelligent people. We do not need to cry for them.

Facts at a Glance

Name	Republic of Argentina
Government Type	Republic
Capital	Buenos Aires
Total Area	1,073,519 square miles (2,766,890 square kilometers)
Climate	Mostly temperate; arid in southeast; sub-Antarctic in the far south
Highest Point	Cerro Aconcagua 22,831 feet (6,960 meters)
Population	37,812,817 (2002 estimate)
Life Expectancy at Birth	74 years (2002 estimate)
Ethnic Groups	White (mostly Spanish and Italian) 97%, mestizo, Native American, or other nonwhite groups 3 percent
Language	Spanish (official), English, Italian, German, French
Religions	Nominally Roman Catholic 92% (less than 20% practicing), Protestant 2%, Jewish 2%, other 4%
Literacy	96%
GDP	$453 billion (2001 estimate)
Natural Resources	Fertile plains of the Pampas, lead, zinc, tin, copper, iron ore, manganese, petroleum, uranium
Industries	Food processing, motor vehicles, consumer durables, textiles, chemicals and petrochemicals, printing, metallurgy, steel
Agricultural Products	Sunflower seeds, lemons, soybeans, grapes, corn, tobacco, peanuts, tea, wheat, livestock
Chief Exports	Edible oils, fuels and energy, cereals, feed, motor vehicles
Chief Imports	Machinery and equipment, motor vehicles, chemicals, metal manufactures, plastics

1516 A.D. Juan Díaz de Solís claims Río de la Plata for Spain.

1580 Spanish settlers establish Buenos Aires.

1776 Spain establishes the Viceroyalty of the Río de la Plata with Buenos Aires as its capital.

1810 Argentina declares independence from Spain.

1829–1852 Juan Manuel de Rosas rules as dictator.

1853 Argentina's constitution is adopted.

1865–1870 War of the Triple Alliance pits Argentina, Brazil, and Uruguay against Paraguay.

1914–1918 The Argentina economy flourishes during World War I.

1929 The Great Depression hits Argentina and a military dictatorship takes control of the country.

1943 Army officers overthrow the government.

1945 Argentina declares war on the Axis powers during World War II.

1946 Juan Domingo Perón is elected president.

1952 President Perón's wife, Eva Duarte de Perón ("Evita"), dies.

1955 The Argentine army and navy revolt and force Perón to flee the country.

1962–1972 A series of civilian presidents and military dictators rule the country.

1973 Perón returns to Argentina and is reelected president.

1976–1983 Argentina's military government conducts the Dirty War, leading to the death of thousands of people.

1982 The United Kingdom defeats Argentina in the Falkland Islands War. Argentina surrenders, but does not give up its claim to the islands.

1994 Terrorists bomb a Jewish community center killing about 30 people.

2002 Congress elects Eduardo Duhalde to be president. Argentina's economy continues to worsen as it default on billions of dollars in debt payments.

Bibliography

Central Intelligence Agency. *CIA Fact Book.* Washington, D.C.: U.S. Government Printing Office, 2002.

Foster, David William, Melissa Fitch Lockhart, and Darrell B. Lockhart. *Culture and Customs of Argentina.* Westport, CT: Greenwood Press, 1998.

Glusberg, Jorge. *Art in Argentina.* Milan, Italy: Giancarlo Politi Editore, 1989.

Hall, Elvajean. *The Land and People of Argentina.* New York: J.B. Lippincott Company, 1960.

Hennessey, Hew. *Insight Guide: Argentina.* Maspeth, NY: Langenscheidt Publishers, Inc., 2000.

Keeling, David J. *Buenos Aires: Global Dreams, Local Crises.* New York: John Wiley & Sons, 1996.

Lewis, Daniel K. *The History of Argentina.* Westport, CN:Greenwood Press, 2001.

Rohter, Larry. "South America Region Under Watch for Signs of Terrorism," *New York Times,* p. 32, December 15, 2002.

Webb, Felicia. "Barely Getting By in Argentina," *New York Times Magazine,* September 1, 2002, pp. 33-34.

Index

Index

Picture Credits

DR. RICHARD A. CROOKER is a geography professor at Kutztown University in Pennsylvania, where he teaches physical geography, oceanography, map reading, and climatology. He received a Ph.D. in Geography from the University of California, Riverside. Dr. Crooker is a member of the Association of American Geographers and the National Council for Geographic Education. He has received numerous research grants, including three from the National Geographical Society. His publications deal with a wide range of geographical topics. He enjoys reading, hiking, bicycling, kayaking, and boogie boarding.

CHARLES F. ("FRITZ") GRITZNER is Distinguished Professor of Geography at South Dakota University in Brookings. He is now in his fifth decade of college teaching and research. During his career, he has taught more than 60 different courses, spanning the fields of physical, cultural, and regional geography. In addition to his teaching, he enjoys writing, working with teachers, and sharing his love for geography with students. As consulting editor for the MODERN WORLD NATIONS series, he has a wonderful opportunity to combine each of these "hobbies." Fritz has served as both president and executive director of the National Council for Geographic Education and has received the Council's highest honor, the George J. Miller Award for Distinguished Service.